Jimmy & Gay —
I wish you the Best
in your marriasing procces
God Bless you Both
Mike Smith

Relationships
The Art of Making Life Work

Relationships
The Art of Making Life Work

John-Roger

Mandeville Press ■ Los Angeles

Published by Mandeville Press
P.O. Box 3935, Los Angeles, CA 90051

Printed by BookCrafters
Chelsea, Michigan
United States of America

I.S.B.N. 0-914829-50-5

Contents

6

SPIRIT   159

Acknowledgements

I wish to acknowledge these people for expressing their loving service with this book: Rick Edelstein-Matisse, editor; Betsy Alexander, copyeditor; Stede Barber, graphics and production manager; Holly Duggan and Janet Bell, proofreaders; and Lynne Wolf, transcriber.

Introduction

All of your relationships are inside of you. Ultimately, each relationship you have with another person reflects your relationship with yourself. How well (or poorly) you get along with yourself will be directly mirrored by how you get along with others inside of you and outside of you.

The cliché is that life is what you make of it, but, in a greater sense, it is what you do with it. Much too often it is your emotional *opinion* about what is going on that is the problem, rather than what is actually happening. Life is designed as a learning experience, not a penalty situation. Rather than being limiting and painful, relationships can be enriching and joyous.

Many people approach today's relationships based on yesterday's lack, precipitating tomorrow's pain. Almost everyone has a history of some form of deprivation, qualifying himself or herself as a leading candidate for the soap opera called life, and many people constantly relate through the drama of their traumas. Influenced by traditional conditioning, most people will not approach relationships based on their own immediate experience. As a result, they may miss out on the thrill of life: abundance, loving, and joy, which are always present for those awake and aware enough to claim them.

This book is offered as a source that you can use to tangibly improve the quality of your life. Each chapter—on marriage, sex, children, communication, your relationship with you, and Spirit—has general and specific information that, if applied, can make your life more joyful. If I have one wish for this book, it is that you use it in such a way as to claim your heritage: a life filled with health, abundance, and loving.

Marriage

Why Marry?

There are many reasons for marriage. Some people get married because they can't stand watching television alone. Others marry because of a need for the sexual expression. Some get married because they're afraid they'll have no one to take care of them when they're old and feeble. Others get married for financial security. Some choose marriage because it's the most acceptable form for having and raising children. Some wed because of parental and social conditioning that says it is the thing to do. Yet others marry to balance past experiences. And some even marry for love.

In many of those situations, people seldom admit—to themselves or to their spouse—their real reasons for marrying. They may marry under the banner of love, but not for the substance. Some remain married for many years with such unspoken thoughts as "is that all there is?" And others may separate with "if that's all there is, I don't want it."

I often suggest to couples that have recently met that they not be in a hurry to marry. I suggest they spend time getting to know each other. How long? A minimum of six months, and I encourage two years. In the first six months the two usually love each other with such infatuation that they automatically cooperate, accept, love, flow, participate, accommodate, nurture, resolve, and share.

In two years, however, some people start expressing negatively, in terms of competing, ignoring, and rejecting. That's the bad news. The good news is that if the couple has been going together for two years, it is easier to conclude the relationship, choosing not to participate in the negativity and learning what they can from the relationship, as they go on their way.

I know couples who have seen an attorney *before* they married in order to work out a contract that defined financial and other elements of their intended relationship, including a detailed account of what would happen in the event of a divorce. Although that may be very practical, it certainly isn't very romantic. But then, does it have to be?

My point of view is that if a couple has to make a legal agreement stipulating conditions for a divorce *before* they are married, why get married? My guideline is, when in doubt, don't do, or when in doubt, talk it out. Marriage, from the point of view of unconditional loving, is difficult enough in a conditioned world. If people get married for the wrong reasons, they are likely to get divorced for the right reasons.

Some people take romance to the extreme and marry thinking that they and their mate are and will always be *everything* to each other. That's a fallacy. Trying to work a marriage on that everything–to–each–other basis is like trying to live in a state of perfection in an imperfect situation. That's not possible because that isn't the way things are designed on this perfectly imperfect planet.

What the marriage is based on will most likely determine the loving or lack of loving expressed, as well as the duration of the relationship.

If a marriage is based only upon the love of sex, it will not last very long—perhaps a year. If, in addition to the sexual expression, each one enjoys the physicality of the other person, that may add a few years to the relationship.

But a marriage based primarily on looking at and making love to each other is limited in terms of time and expression.

Then there are marriages based on emotions. Part of this can be staying married for the sake of the children, and after the children are gone, there can often be divorce. An emotionally based marriage will last longer if it includes mental love. What does a couple do after the children are gone and they feel less desire for the sexual expression? A marriage including mental love, where a couple loves to talk and share, can wonderfully last a lifetime.

If you get married because you are in love, then know that you can just as easily be out of love. If you get married because you love your mate for what he or she will do, then you may not love them if they don't do what you want or expect. But if you marry simply because you love the other person and it doesn't matter what they do, then that is the marriage that can endure and be enjoyed throughout all experiences for a lifetime.

In those marriages where the unconditional, spiritual love is present, total love on all levels is likely, including a harmonious balance of the mental, emotional, physical, and sexual expressions. You live together in a natural state of living love. This is closest to the happily–ever–after fantasy.

Is That Who I Married?

After two people commit to a relationship and begin living together, they can't help but become involved with the intimacies of day-to-day living: the humdrum of paying bills, the occasional aches and pains that sometimes come with events in the relationship, and the sexual pleasures and pressures. More than one married couple has been involved in a conversation like this:

"We only made love twice this week."

"Once, but who's counting?"

"You just didn't make a move toward me."

"Well, you can reach out, too."

"I did last time. It's your turn to reach out."

"No, you didn't. *I* was the one who reached out last time."

In this form of relating, they start to reveal to their loved one different parts of themselves that are far from perfect. In fact, they may be so far from perfect that these things were kept well-hidden during the romancing (courting) period. Then, when a person feels secure enough with their spouse, they may drop the act (role playing) and reveal what was hidden.

Of course, if they had been smart and courageous at the beginning, they'd have revealed that *before* the marriage. If they didn't, they may have to face the pressure of change. When the imperfections are revealed in the marriage, quite often each partner wants the other to change, to alter their behavior or attitudes. After all, not many people want to live with imperfections, especially if they're someone else's.

Sometimes it may be for your benefit to look at your mate's concept of you and see if it is accurate or just their conditioned eyes focusing on your imperfections. Just because your mate may see lack of loving in all kinds of things you do and don't do, as the song goes, "It ain't necessarily so." Their experience of you may be closer to their experience of a loss from their past rather than the reality of what is.

While you don't have to accept someone else's experience of you, it would be for your advancement to look at it and make sure you are not defending a position out of ego. If you honestly look at what is really going on and remain in touch with your affection for your partner, it will be easier for you to act with loving support. It's a matter of doing what it takes to get the necessary altitude to see what is really going on; then your attitude and actions of loving support and humor are an easy result.

There's Gonna Be Some Changes Made

When couples don't have enough experience or will-power to go for the positive, they often have won't-power and point out all the things that are supposedly wrong with the other person.

It can get downright nasty, to the point of one saying, "If I had known you were like that, I wouldn't have married you." The honest response might be, "I knew that, which is why I didn't let you know." Then each of them is faced with the challenge of loving the other enough (with all that they do know) to look at the imperfections through the eyes of love.

Some people may stick to the traditional struggle: "I'll love you only if you change." If the response is, "I won't change until you change," the couple may be stuck with that. Another response might be, "Why must I change? Why can't I just have that imperfection, and we continue to relate in loving anyway?" The choice, then, is to go for that or to stay stuck in an emotional reaction of "because when you do that, it makes me sick."

It could be time for you to get in touch with that sick feeling and see if it has as much to do with the other person as it does with cultural conditioning that is giving birth to judgment. In other words, your *background* might be clouding your *foreground*.

5

Imperfections don't always have to be regarded as the bad news. The good news is that human frailties and imperfections are often shared only when a person relaxes enough not to edit their thoughts, habits, or feelings.

For example, imagine having the courage to admit, "You're the only one who can hurt me, and you're the only one I've ever trusted enough to show these things. I know I need help, but you want me to change before I know what I'm dealing with and how to change it. You're ready to walk out the door before I've even begun to look at a habit I developed long before I met you. Can't we sit and look at it? Maybe I can change it if I know what I'm going to change. Not change just to please you, but change the formula that caused it. And that takes some looking, some investigation, some knowing that lets me get in touch with it."

It is the inability to get in touch with a habitual response that makes it so difficult to change. It's like trying to open a combination lock without turning the dial. No matter how much you theorize, until you actually get in there and start experimenting to find out what the process is, you can't come close to unlocking the habit.

In loving—*real* loving, which is unconditional—you can assist your lover rather than criticize or issue ultimatums. Rather than a change–or–else attitude, a supportive approach of loving no matter what will encourage adjustments.

What do you think will be produced by the attitude of "I'm going to marry you, but you have to change"? Probably not change. Or if there is change, it may be accompanied by resentment because the change came about as a result of intimidation or coercion. If you issue a change–or–else ultimatum, at best you may end up with a change *and* an "or else," the "or else" being resentment.

You might think, "Well, if I don't demand the change, I'm stuck with the behavior that makes me crazy." Again, maybe it's your responsibility to get in touch with what makes you crazy. "My spouse's behavior" may be your immediate response, but I would bet that you have that get-crazy button pushed and set off by people other than just your spouse. Get in touch with it. It's your button that is being pushed. Instead of trying to change the button pushers so quickly, how about removing the button itself or changing your response when the button is pushed?

You can always leave your loved one in your righteous indignation. This will leave you open to find another person to love, who will most likely test and bless you with even greater imperfections that push the it–makes–me–crazy button harder and more often. If this happens, you're likely to leave that relationship even quicker than the previous one.

It's important for your relationship that you do not treat your mate's *problem* as more important than your *mate*. I don't care what the nature of the problem is. Problems are to be dealt with, but don't make the mistake of thinking that the problems *are* your husband or your wife. Your loved one is bigger than the problem. You can assist your mate in avoiding inappropriate behavior as long as you communicate that you love him or her more than the issue of concern.

I know of one husband who experiences great stress at work and needs time to unwind when he comes home. Sometimes, before he has had sufficient time to relax, his wife or his children may demand some attention that he's not yet ready to give. He often responds irritably, to the point of anger and impatience. His wife and children know him, and they usually just laugh. "That's Daddy. Give him 15 more minutes, scratch his head, and he'll be back to normal." You see, you don't always have to react to someone's frailty or even demand that they change. Some can even be observed, tolerated, and laughed with, if you will.

Sexual Fidelity, Fantasies, and Frequency

Inherent in most committed relationships is the understanding that each of you will have sex only with the other. If this is not clear in each of your minds and hearts, please be sure to talk about it.

When the sexual expression is a loving, intimate, physical gesture of affection, it will normally contribute loving, positive energy to a couple. If there is deceit involved in that area, however, negativity can be received into your being, and the natural energy can be depleted. Deceit in the sexual area can cause distress, disease, and divorce.

I encourage couples to be honest with each other in sharing their intent regarding sexual fidelity and in living up to their agreement; if the agreement is changed on either side, the partner is to be notified right away.

Actually, if you have come to a reluctant agreement in a bartering, give–and–take session, you might want to take a good, long, hard look at your relationship. If you feel that making love only to your mate is a restriction, you may be involved in the wrong kind of relationship. Perhaps it might be better if you two were not together, because if you are involved in a loving, committed relationship, the natural, preferred expression is fidelity. The sexual expression of love, shared only between two committed lovers, is what making love is all about. Anything less is distracting; anything more can be harmful.

It doesn't matter all that much if you feel lust when you see an attractive man or woman other than your mate.

What does matter is whether you let this lust run you; it matters what you're going to do with it when it does appear.

Some people choose to have an affair with that other person, justifying it by saying they're getting lust out of their system. Maybe so, but they may also be getting *into* their system other things: guilt, remorse, despair, feelings of betrayal, and even degradation.

That hell which is part of betrayal fulfills the saying "your sins have found you out," because your guilt may punish you more than the mere sexual act. You may be further ahead not to give in to lust under any rationale. If you do choose it, then do it knowingly, accepting all that comes with it and owning your behavior.

It's a matter of learning discipline and self-control instead of giving in to a primal lust that disappears a minisecond after the act and keeps reemerging again and again and again because it can never be satisfied. Being a slave to an unquenchable thirst is not a very smart way to live.

There are some people who think they can get away with it. They're convinced that if they take such care that their mate does not discover them, no one will be the wiser and no one will be hurt. There is always a knower. It's in yourself, certainly, and your body, emotions, and life experiences will reflect such a betrayal no matter what rationale you offer.

There is also your perceptive mate. He or she may not know specifically what has happened, but there very well might be some intuitive recording that may root deeply as separation in your relationship. Perhaps someday this root may spring forth and grow into something like divorce when your mate says, "I found another lover." It's called "chickens come home to roost" or "as you sow, so shall you reap."

If you already know that making love and later falling

asleep with your mate is the only way to go, you have a good start on a loving, lasting relationship.

A husband or wife may sometimes fantasize another person in their arms as they are making love to their mate. Perhaps without knowing it, the one who is fantasizing is pushing the other away. If you do this, you may be either making love because of pressure and expectations (thus creating the fantasy in order to perform) or having sex more often than you'd prefer. You may be having sex (rather than making love) to prove yourself because of an unconscious insecurity about your gender or relationship.

If you are not sexually stimulated by the person who is present at the moment, I encourage you *not* to create a fantasy in order to justify and fulfill the act. The person—your lover, your wife, or your husband—is the one who is present, and both of you deserve all of your attention (physical, emotional, mental, imaginative, and spiritual) during the highly charged sexual expression.

Your lover is a pearl of great price. Don't use sex only as "casual recreation" with someone so precious. Instead, you can use sex as one form of intimacy and sharing. In that context a recharging and oneness evolve as each of you becomes secure with the other and with yourselves as a couple. That is a most comfortable form of togetherness.

You don't have to use sexual intercourse in order to be sexual, sensual, or romantic. You can share a shower or a massage, lie with each other and listen to music that opens the heart, cuddle, and fall asleep. That, too, is romance.

When a couple shifts from the courting period to marriage, the sexual expression often changes, becoming less romantic, less charged, and usually less frequent. Don't worry or judge yourself or your partner if this occurs. It is part of the qualitative and quantitative change that often takes place with increased physical proximity and a committed relationship. There are seldom concerns of "will she?" or "is he?" Part of the built-in condition of your marriage is an expectation that the sexual expression will be available.

Let the change be all right. Let the fact that you may romance each other differently be permissible. That is not to say that you should be inconsiderate or mechanical. No. Never forget that the sexual expression is called lovemaking. Make sure that no matter how, where, or when, you are making *love* to and with your mate.

Many animals have mating periods, and some people say that this is not the case with human beings. I'm not so sure about that. In my observation and counselings with couples who have been married from 2 to 20 years, I have found out that people do go through sexual cycles.

There seem to be recurring periods when individual men and women are not as sexually assertive or not as receptive to the sexual act. This is not to say that the loving diminishes. Not at all. It is just part of nature's cycle that the expression is not always on "high." You don't need to judge or feel guilty about this. Just become aware of your own particular rhythm and share your awareness with your mate.

One of the worst things a couple can do is go to bed with pressure and sleep with unresolved discomfort. If the man reaches out and the woman says "not tonight, honey" often enough and without a heart-to-heart discussion, the man may stop reaching out to her, and eventually he may go out to reach—out of the house. The same thing holds if a woman wants to make love and the man doesn't want to turn off the eleven o'clock news on TV. If the man does that often enough, his wife may be the one making the news.

I suggest that you share lovingly, candidly, and intimately. Know that it is not only all right, but it is more usual than people will admit, that there are high and low sexual cycles. If such is the case for you on occasion, you can share this with your partner: "Honey, I'm crazy in love with you, and I'm going through a period where I just want to fall asleep holding you. I don't know what it is, but I love you and I just don't feel like sex. It may just be a cycle, and it has nothing to do with the fact that I deeply love you."

That kind of loving honesty makes it much easier for a man or a woman to handle sexual cycles. In the sharing, there is no feeling of rejection, blame, or guilt. Then, indeed, you can both go to sleep lovingly, knowing that sexual cycles are normal—not good or bad, but just part of nature.

They're Playing Our Song

Endearing experiences and expressions occur between two people in a committed relationship. Sometimes a song becomes a precious event during their courtship. My advice is that you don't dissipate that value by sharing it as "special" with someone else.

Similarly, if you end up calling your loved one an endearing, caressing term, don't use that expression with anyone else. Whether it is as common as "honey," "sweetheart," or "baby," if you use that term for your "honey," make sure you keep that energy sacred to each other by reserving that term for your loved one.

It's a security blanket to have those things, those words, those songs, those private places that only you two share.

Kiss and Touch, or Is Anything Sacred?

Just because you want to be free and without restrictions doesn't mean that you don't have sensitivity, respect, and responsibility. Those considerations are not intended to dissolve just because you marry and, in effect, fall into an intimate relationship. I suggest you *rise* to the relationship rather than fall.

There are some things that are sacred to some people—some expressions in which privacy is preferred— some behavior that is intended only for your intimate sharing with your mate. What those things are varies according to culture, gender, and individuals. They are for you to determine with your partner in respect and appreciation and, most of all, loving acceptance.

There are ways that couples kiss and touch, even in public, that are subtly sacred to each other; keep that expression limited to the privacy of you two. For example, I know a man who, when he was single, always kissed women on the lips as a form of greeting. It was casual and affectionate, and he said it didn't really mean anything. Yet, after talking about it more honestly, he admitted that it was a subtle form of flirting.

When he got married, he and his wife realized there was some insecurity in the way each of them related to other men and women. He felt that she flirted, and she did. She felt that he made himself too available for women to hug and kiss and pat, and he did.

After about six months of struggling in this area, getting past their egos and habits, each of them surrendered. It went like this:

"Honey, I just don't want men to pat you on the backside, even if you have known them for ten years."

"I agree," she responded. "It doesn't feel comfortable for me any longer. I'll make sure they don't." And she did—not by hanging out a sign, but just by not being available to it. Most people are sensitive and get that. Every now and then, someone would be thick and insensitive and would reach out. She would then make herself clear, with words and by grabbing his hand: "Thank you, but that area's just for my husband."

She also said to her husband, "Darling, I just don't like it when all those women friends of yours kiss you on the lips and hug you and hold their body against you as if I didn't exist."

He replied, "Neither do I." And he turned the other cheek. Literally.

This couple could have dug into a concept of freedom and said, "I love you, and my kissing or being patted has nothing to do with my love for you. That's just the way I express myself. If you interpret it negatively, that's for you to deal with." Watch out for the words that sound so good and justify everything but loving consideration.

The couple I'm talking about surrendered to consideration, not to ego. They made certain parts of their bodies and actions sacred to them, weaving their security blanket together.

Success–full Marriage

Most people would probably say that a successful marriage is based on unconditional loving. The truth is, however, that people usually don't marry because of unconditional loving; they marry for conditioned loving. Conditions are presented to each other, including that they love one another unconditionally, based upon conditions. They often demand that the other person fill that empty, lonely, insecure space inside of them, and the person simply doesn't know how to do that. No one knows how to fill up anybody else regardless of all the romantic songs and movies. In fact, very few know how to fill up themselves.

Rather than attempt to be unconditionally loving 100 percent of the time and demand that your lover be in a similar state "or else," I suggest that each of you choose the experience that exists in the moment. By choosing, I mean accepting what is going on with no judgment, blame, or ultimatum.

If something is bothering you about his or her behavior, you can change your focus rather than get upset. Doing this requires commitment and inner discipline. In fact, marriage, in order to be successful, requires 100 percent commitment to loving—commitment, not necessarily accomplishment. In other words, if your partner sometimes exhibits less–than–loving behavior, don't beat them over the head with, "But you agreed to 100 percent commitment!"

Commitment really means that you both go for 100 percent loving. Don't expect perfection because it may not be available, and the paradox is that you still go for it. The best you'll end up with is excellence, and excellence in loving is almost totally fulfilling.

What will eliminate the "almost" and actually bring fulfillment is the other element necessary to a success–full relationship: total acceptance of the other. Accepting all the positive attributes is easy. How about accepting the human frailties, *without judgment, resentment, or disappointment?* (Judgment, by the way, is an attempt to get people to think you are perfect. When someone is perfect, the implication is that they have the right to judge. Actually, however, in the perfected state, there is no judgment because you can see that all is, indeed, perfect.)

In any situation, get beyond the words to the heart because if the heart is not heard, no words can really help. Once into the heart (yours and your lover's), then you can give and receive, lift and be lifted. If you're not loving and caring for each other, there is really no need to be together.

You can go through junk and disagreements together, as long as you are both committed to going through and getting through the junk, together. The more you both do that, the quicker you will get through it until, ultimately, that junkyard will be history, a historic frame of reference for yourself and others.

In order to make your marriage work, first go within yourself and make a secure and safe place for each of you. (Safety and security are products accompanied by liberal doses of the following ingredients: compassion, acceptance, humor, and a double helping of love.)

To make marriage work, you also have to continue to get married, every day. In fact, it might be called "marriaging," an ongoing activity of nourishing and caring for each other.

I know two people very much in love. After observing them for three years, I've seen that their love is more joyous and humorous than ever before. Why? Because they are marriag*ing.* They keep the relationship alive by acts that are accepting and nourishing. Here is an example of something that happened with them recently:

One day, while driving to a movie, the man felt that his wife was separating from him. It wasn't anything she said or did, but when you are deeply in love and experienced with a person, you can often intuit something without obvious indications. He asked his wife, "Is anything wrong?"

She said, "No, I'm just quiet."

When they parked the car he still felt the separation. Again he said, "Are you sure everything's all right?"

She said, "Yes, I just need to be alone for a little while."

His initial reaction was anger, tension, and all those other emotional–hurt buttons. After all, they had planned to go to a movie and to have a pizza and a wonderful day together. Yet here she was, separating.

He was aware of his emotions starting to rise, but chose not to give energy to those feelings and thoughts. He just said, "How long do you want to be alone?"

She said, "About 15 or 20 minutes."

He said, "Okay. The movie doesn't start for 30 minutes. I'll meet you in front of the theater in 20 minutes." And he left her in the car.

The woman remained in the car, spending time alone with herself. She didn't understand what was going on, nor did she judge it. She simply gave herself permission to be with her thoughts, her feelings, and whatever else came up. She sat there and indulged in just being, a beautiful gift.

As for him, while walking he went through moments of experiencing rejection, anger, and isolation. Then he got distracted from those emotions by people-watching and window-shopping, and he started to enjoy being alone. Eventually he found himself in front of a flower store. "What the heck," he thought, "so she needs to be alone. I'm having a great time, and I'm crazy about her, so I'm going to surprise her with flowers."

That's just what he did. He bought her three roses (one white, one yellow, and one purple) and managed to put them in his back pocket, so when he saw her she wouldn't immediately see the flowers.

She was waiting for him in front of the theater, having done whatever it was she needed to do to balance herself. She was now ready to be with him, and she hugged him. Then she felt something sticking out of his back pocket. The discovery of his loving gift of flowers permitted them both to laugh and enjoy as they went into the theater, and now their relationship is even richer than before. (Incidentally, they told me the movie was terrible and they laughed all the way through it, having a great time.)

That's a living example of people who chose a positive, loving expression in the midst of negative temptation. They chose to go for the loving rather than the emotional upset.

You don't have to lay your annoyance on your mate. Instead, how about saying, "I've married you, and you can continue on just like you are if that's what you want, because there's no demand from me to change. If I get annoyed when you do something, we'll both know it, and I'll make it my responsibility to love you through my annoyance."

In time, your annoyance might change to amusement and acceptance of your loved one's all–too–human conditioning. (Changing the attitude is a great key to having constructive, long–lasting, loving relationships.) When you show that kind of unconditional loving, such a secure support may encourage your lover to change that habit just because of loving understanding. Not pressure. And even if they don't change, you are still experiencing love because you have chosen love.

Making Your Own Movie

You are actually the writer, the director, and the star of your own movie. It's called *This Is Your Life*. Is it a comedy? A romantic drama? A horror picture? A soap opera? How do you view your own movie?

There are many ways you can view a film. For instance, you can go to a movie and choose to be scared to death by what you see and hear. That's perpetuating an artificial relationship. If you want the true relationship, you agree that it is a movie, images shown on a screen, an artificial device that is *not* life, and you agree to this when you buy a ticket. Parts of the film—within that agreed relationship—may be amusing, scary, or uninteresting, and all of that is fine because you agreed to the relationship.

The same thing can exist in personal, intimate relationships. In essence, when you commit, you are buying a ticket to the great movie called *Relationships*. Depending upon your agreement, it can be amusing, scary, uninteresting, fascinating, enriching, inspiring, and any number of other things. The important thing to remember is that you are the one who "bought the ticket" to the relationship movie. You are the one who chooses to be the romantic lead, the comedy relief, the star–crossed ingenue, the hero, the villain, the victor, or the victim. It is all up to you and your attitude. Once you know that, you can commit to the relationship you have with your lover, rather than avoid it by judging and by making them wrong and you right.

The relationship movie may be about God's sense of humor. It may be filled with tenderness, absurdity, compassion, pain, and loving.

Do Children Add or Subtract?

When a child is born into a family, there is a substantial adjustment necessary for the adults. They add new roles to the ones of husband and wife; they are now also father and mother. This adjustment is best approached with awareness and sensitivity. If you have children, make sure that you care enough for yourself, your spouse, and your children to balance your lives.

This is easier said than done. To those who are unprepared, it is as if the world turned upside down for them. Usually the woman may be more prepared, perhaps because she has carried the child, and the gestation period may foster an organic relationship by the time the child is born. The man may be less prepared because he continues to have most of his wife's attention during that nine–month period. Then, all of a sudden, much of his wife's attention is called elsewhere.

When an infant is born, energy is focused on that being, who needs so much physical attention and certainly a great deal of loving, understanding, guidance, and support. Much of this effort is expressed by the mother. That is not to say that the father cannot participate fully. It can often be advantageous for both parents to share in the work and loving, from changing diapers to feeding to rocking to playing.

However, it is the female who carries and gives birth, and it is also the mother who nurses the child (when a bottle is not being used). The mother is often the parent who spends time with the child while the father continues to work and earn funds to pay for the necessities and luxuries in their lives. The mother is often the one who awakens to feed the baby in the middle of the night in order that the father can get enough sleep to work during the day.

The paradox is that the mother works during the day, too, within a different schedule. She is spending a great deal of time taking care of their infant and, if she's smart, taking naps when the baby does.

Here is a possible scenario: By the time the father comes home, the mother has changed the baby's diapers about a dozen times, washed and dried a load or two of laundry, cooked a meal, cleaned a house, and talked to the infant in baby talk. She is usually exhausted.

The father has worked all day, dealt with issues, concerns, and conflicts with his boss and colleagues, balanced them as best he could, driven home in bumper–to–bumper traffic, and he is usually exhausted.

The mother wants to put the baby to sleep, eat, relax, and have the husband/father talk with her. She needs the lover in him. She needs the husband–adult to share, care, and express affection and loving. She's been giving all day, and now she just needs to relax and receive.

The husband/father is a little irritable from the office concerns, the traffic, and the unpaid bills; in the midst of this, he picks up the baby, who wets him. He really wants to put the baby to sleep, be served a meal, relax by watching TV, and fall asleep, forgetting about the world. He just needs to relax and receive.

What do you think the baby wants? At this age, the child is on automatic, wanting food, stroking, affection, care, and comfort. In other words, the baby just wants to relax and receive.

So there you have it—three living beings in the same house at the same time, all wanting to relax and receive. Hardly a giver in the crowd.

If they go the traditional route—meaning lack of awareness—they will blame each other for not giving. Of course, the infant isn't expected to have awareness and will probably cry and fuss when attention is not forthcoming. Then the parents may get even more irritable, and the baby may cry and fuss even more.

The husband/father might say to the wife/mother, "Will you put your kid to bed, already!"

The wife/mother can automatically respond, "It's your kid, too. How about you putting her to bed."

"I've been working all day."

"What do you think I've been doing?"

"Watching soap operas."

"Oh, yeah? I was washing out dirty diapers while you were having a martini for lunch." *Ad infinitum, ad absurdum*, ad divorce 'em.

Those early months with an infant can be difficult; it's a delicate balance. I suggest that you two lovers—yes, *lovers*—be aware that you started out as lovers and avoid the traditional trap of over–identifying with the mother–father syndrome. You can do what it takes to make sure that adult loving–time is alive and well. Of course, it will be quantitatively different than before. Taking care of an infant takes enormous physical, emotional, and spiritual energy, particularly from the mother. The male lover will do well to keep that in mind and to appreciate her expression to their child.

It can be a difficult time for the man, too. The lover in him is used to having "his woman" available to love, to care for, to give to and receive from, and to play with spontaneously. Now, with the child demanding so much energy, a source of joy in his life (his wife) is not as available as she was before. Sometimes the man feels a sense of loss, as if he has lost his wife to his child. Sometimes he also experiences resentment and guilt—resentment because of the quantitative loss of his lover and guilt because he resents this while simultaneously recognizing that she is a great mother to his great child.

A revolution in priorities has taken place with the birth of the child. For example, there will be times when the lovers are expressing their affection sexually and the infant wakes up and starts crying. A revolution in priorities may call for the sexual act to be put on hold. (It's very difficult to make sexual love when a loved infant is crying and needs care.)

In spite of these difficulties and adjustments, the birth of a child is a great opportunity for the lovers/parents. They can both be part of the birth in many ways. Certainly, the physical birth can be attended and supported by the father, too, but I am talking more about a new birth in understanding, awareness, and sensitivity, birth to a new level of caring from adult to adult.

The caring can manifest in both grand and prosaic ways. On his way home, for example, the man can make the effort and buy some flowers and Chinese food. The woman can chill a drink for her husband and herself as she is warming a bottle of milk. A baby–sitter can be arranged so the parents can have separate adult-time with each other.

During those times when you don't feel comfortable leaving the infant with a baby–sitter (the child may have a cold or a temperature), you can still sit around together, make some popcorn, watch a silly TV show, and rub your lover's back. When the child whimpers, you can say, "I'll get it, honey. You just tell me what happened when I get back." And when your lover gets back, you share the end of the TV show, rub your lover's temples, and fall asleep with each other in that loving state.

Being a parent can be an exquisite, extraordinary miracle that can work. You are a crucial part of bringing a human being onto this planet for a life experience. The experience can be a pleasure, a loving joy, and a great strengthener. For all three of you. Or four. Or more.

You lovers who are also parents can avoid the trap of making your life all about your child to the point of causing separation between each other. Your child is an expression of your life—a very important one. However, if you don't live your life in loving with each other, as adults, your child will pay the dues for that relationship. When loving is not expressed between the parents, the child experiences the loss.

You can have it all. Love and support each other as lovers, and appreciate your roles as mother and father. Loving and supporting your child is easy after that and only adds to your life as you all nurture one another.

Pain, the Awakener

When we give up our rights as individuals to other people, we are potentially opening the door to pain. In the traditional marriage vows of many years ago, the woman promised to "love, honor, and obey" her husband. The word *obey* connotes one consciousness being subservient to another, and any form of slavery can create resentment and pain.

Similarly, the marriage vows of "for better or for worse, for richer or for poorer" intimate responsibilities that you may be incapable of handling. Certainly, the "poorer . . . worse" parts are not your preference. A more aware preference might be that each one not be a parasite or a leech upon the other, but be two people working together in mutual respect, cooperation, and lots of loving, with a liberal dash of humor to get through the difficult times.

Within a marriage, whenever your loved one takes any action, you are tied in some way to that action. For example, if the wife gets in debt, the husband has to pay the bill. If the husband bangs up his wife's car, her insurance company has to support the claim.

Instead of the romantic version of a marriage being two people head over heels in love with each other, staring blissfully into each other's eyes, I suggest a greater reality: two people looking in the same direction—not at each other—sharing a life path that can enrich and support both.

Another metaphor might be the husband as a pine tree and the wife as an oak tree. Neither can grow in the shadow of the other. They both have to stand far enough apart so the roots of one don't strangle the roots of the other. As they get taller, an intermingling and sharing of beauty may take place, but at the bottom, where the stability lies, each must establish their own roots and foundation. You'd be further ahead to avoid the romantic fantasy and go for the reality. If you don't, you may create pain with the other and, certainly, for yourself.

People think that the easiest thing to do, in the short run, is to try to escape from pain, using whatever means possible: drugs; meaningless sex; excess food, alcohol or cigarettes; excessive time spent with television, books, or films—anything to get away from the pain, right? Because after all, why hang around in the pain that someone else is causing, right?

In the long run, however, trying to escape from pain is like trying to run away from yourself; it can't be done. You can go wherever you want, but the pain goes with you because pain is the response mechanism within you.

You may think, "But it's because of them. That's why I run away. I want to get away from them!" Of course, there may be times when it may be a wise choice not to be with those individuals who are expressing negativity. There may also be times when other choices may be even more beneficial to your growth. You might adopt another attitude and consider the possibility that someone else isn't the cause of your pain. Although it may seem as if your spouse is causing the pain by doing a certain thing, there is always another way of looking at the situation: just as the source of love is within you, so is the source of pain. When you experience pain, it is coming from a pain–full source *within you*.

You still might say, "I don't get it." My reply would be, "Yes, you do; you get your pain, but it isn't always your spouse's fault." Many people I know have been married and divorced numerous times and have had similar difficulties with each new marriage because it's the same old pattern. Their own negativity carried into each new relationship, and they perpetuated the pain by blaming the other.

Pain is just a method of recognition. Some people are willing to look, but few have the courage to see. If you are brave enough to see, you might recognize that the pain you are experiencing has more to do with you than with him or her. By placing the blame on him or her, you can be attempting to avoid the relationship within yourself.

I knew someone who used to go through anxiety attacks before a sporting event involving a favorite team. That person experienced extreme pain or pleasure, depending upon the outcome of the game. I experienced none of those things in relationship to the same event. Was it the team that caused my friend's pain or pleasure?

If it was, then I should have had the same experience. It appeared to be a matter of each individual's attitude. It is clear that my friend's personal relationship with the event included emotional importance placed on the outcome of the game. My relationship to the same game was quite different. I didn't care who won or lost, yet I could enjoy watching the game.

Years later, I ran into this same friend and asked, "When that team loses, does it still drive you up the wall?" My friend responded, "No. Not anymore. I've outgrown that."

"Outgrown that" is very accurate. In other words, he needed to grow in order to recognize that his emotional reaction was his to own; in owning it, he could also discard it.

The same thing applies to your intimate relationship. When your spouse does that thing that can drive you up the wall, you can choose to outgrow it—not your spouse's action, but your reaction. You can do this if you are willing to own your reaction.

Owning it is another step toward awakening. Many people have allowed themselves to live a life in sleep. They seem to be walking through a nightmare of conditioned influences from their mother, father, society, gender expectations, financial background, sexual anticipations, fears, and everything but their original selves. We may as well face it: the history of planet Earth has not been seen as conducive to supporting original, loving, joyous abundance. Yet it is available for every individual who has the courage to go for it. How?

Certainly not by blaming or by making *them* wrong or the source of your pain. In order to awaken and activate the original you, you can start by accepting that the primary relationship in your life is with yourself. You can also realize that each of your emotional responses is yours to own and that *you* determine your attitude. What power you have! What a magnificent being you are! Are you willing and courageous enough to claim it?

Jealousy in Marriage

Jealousy works similarly to many other self–defense mechanisms, integrating many parts and precipitating an emotional reaction. If you try to handle just one part of the mechanism, it is usually ineffective. For instance, if you are jealous because you think your mate is flirting with someone else and if you divorce, in your next marriage, you may very well have to face a similar concern because of your intricate mechanisms.

It would serve you to first fix your "inner gears" that have become so well–oiled toward jealousy. Then, if someone does behave in a manner that doesn't work for you, you can deal with it as *information*, rather than through automatic emotional reactions to the mechanisms of the mind.

Jealousy is a process of vision, self–image, and imagination stemming from a weak self–concept. From that place of "I'm not really good enough" and "once my act is perceived, my mate will see my true lack of worthiness," you can create an image that supports that position of lack.

27

Jealousy is found primarily in the love relationships of an individual who is experiencing a lack–of–love relationship with himself or herself. Until a person does whatever it takes to recognize their true worth and value, every relationship can be hurt by jealousy. If people don't keep focused on the loving, they may fall into jealous accusations, often without proof, but with righteous emotion.

The dynamics of jealousy reveal not only a person's lack of trust for someone else but also a lack of trust for himself or herself. The fear that they will lose their lover's love or that their lover will love someone else more is a driving force. Jealousy is a highly destructive force involving paranoia as a support system.

I have known extraordinary behavior from people trying to justify the jealousy that was actually covering their own unreliable behavior or their own insecurity, which has nothing to do with the other person's experience. For example, I know of one husband who came home late from work, and when he went to flush the toilet, he noticed two cigarettes. He actually reached into the bowl (in which he had relieved himself) to pull the urine–soaked cigarettes out in order to determine if the brand was his wife's.

I know of a wife who, when working late in the office, received a call from her husband, asking what time she was coming home. She thought, "He never calls and asks that. He must have another woman in our house. Our bedroom. Our bed!"

She ran out before she finished the report she promised to have for her boss in the morning. She drove through the city like she was competing in the Indianapolis 500 race, barely missing a major accident. Two blocks before she got home, she turned off the car lights, and one block away, she put the gears in neutral so her husband wouldn't hear her arrive.

At the front door, she took off her shoes, tiptoed into the house, and then went directly into the bedroom, ready to catch them. No one was there. She heard a cork pop in the kitchen. "Ahh," she thought, "they're having a drink in the kitchen. Probably from that favorite wine we've been saving for a special occasion!"

She stormed into the kitchen—almost causing her husband to have a heart attack in surprise—only to find him there, fixing dinner for her. He had called her so he would have the surprise dinner all ready by the time she came home.

The wife was still stuck in jealousy as she said, "How did you get her out of here so fast? I can smell her perfume. How come you're cooking? Feeling guilty?" These acts are also like paranoia.

The best way to handle these feelings of jealousy may be to share them with your mate, in honest vulnerability, *not* in accusation. You take responsibility for your feelings.

I know of one man who did that with his wife, and she just smiled and hugged him for caring so much. She sat near him, assuring him how much she loved him, and said, "Ask me any questions, darling, if you are still concerned about why I was late." In that simple way of giving him permission to ask, she diffused the concern. He asked, she answered, he felt better and apologized, and she just loved him for caring so much and being honest.

A woman can see a good–looking man and enjoy his appearance, and a man may appreciate something about another woman. They can enjoy and appreciate, but not participate, and if that is shared, even gender concerns can be transcended. For example, a couple can appreciate the beauty of another woman or another man, in person, on television, in the movies, or in a magazine. You can even play with each other about it with humor. If you're not going to have humor in your marriage, I suggest you re-examine your relationship because very few things on this planet can last without humor. Humor is often the only release from tension that cannot be resolved intellectually.

You can't cure jealousy by logical reasoning because it's not a logical, reasoning process. You and your partner have to demonstrate trust and unconditional loving by behavior. If you're unwilling to do that, you can be run by jealousy. If you two are physically separated, you don't have to imagine that your partner is involved with someone else. Instead, how about imagining that he or she is involved in some beautiful, loving, supportive action. Physical separation does not have to mean separation in loving.

Instead of giving in to the devious mechanisms of jealousy, as soon as it starts you can activate your awareness and choices. Don't let jealousy become just another habitual response.

Do what it takes to improve your own self-image. Do those things that give you an experience of your worth. These could include such things as ballet lessons, aerobics classes, study of a foreign language, photography, greater expressions in service to the community—whatever works for you.

Jealousy cannot survive in an atmosphere of worthiness, appreciation, and love. Instead of trying to solve the effect of jealousy, you can eliminate the cause by strengthening yourself.

Tricks That Work

How do you keep the loving going on a practical one-to-one relating level when things get sticky? (And there will probably be times when they do, indeed, get sticky, if not downright rough.) In other words, how do you translate the concept of unconditional loving into living actions? When things are hellish, how do you invoke heaven?

Practice. Use any- and everything to get yourself into that active, loving state. Besides such things as contemplation, meditation, spiritual exercises, workshops, seminars, uplifting literature, and so on, you can invent your own methods.

Some people use a symbol on a necklace that indicates loving. Others have a ring. Some have something in their pocket that was a precious gift of love, or they may even wear a rubber band on their wrists that they snap as a stinging reminder to avoid negativity. Of course, these are only physical objects, which have no inherent power. They are, however, symbols of your intention; they are your methods, your reminder.

I have seen people use those physical objects when the pressure is on. When you are inclined to go for one of those "you–said–I–said–you–did–I–did" routines, making the other person wrong and exploding in righteous indignation, take a second and just physically touch that object. In that physical touch, think of the loving it represents. Run your anger and your emotional reaction through that object, and see if it dissolves. You can use that inanimate object to reawaken your loving power. Does it work? It can, if you work it.

You've heard the expression "count to ten before you talk," meaning do what it takes while you're in an emotional state to center yourself. That actually works for some people. Others have to count to one hundred before they get centered. Some people have a word or a phrase that they repeat silently when they get into one of those "off-center" states. If you choose such a key word or phrase, it's best to choose something when you are flowing with love. Then that word or expression will naturally have the loving energy. When you call on it during an upset period and repeat it as long as is necessary to receive of the loving energy, your emotional upset can be transformed into neutral observation, acceptance, and even warm, human love. A trick? Perhaps, but anything that evokes loving has value.

One person I know uses a particular piece of music (Pablo Casals playing Bach on the cello), which immediately cools him out, soothes him, and helps him reconnect to his beautifully loving heart.

Find those tricks that work for you, and then work them. Living on this planet is sometimes tricky. Why not be a great magician? Be an alchemist, and transform negativity into loving. It's possible. You can even involve your mate in this technique, and you both may play the love-trick game.

I know two lovers who received a pair of beautiful Dresden figurines as a wedding gift. They kept these dolls on a table in the bedroom. If one person was upset or angry with the other, that one would go into the bedroom and turn one doll so its back was to the other.

When the other went to the bedroom and saw this, they recognized there was a problem. Of course, a traditionally conditioned person might turn the other doll around so there would be two dolls with their backs to each other, imitating two human beings.

Fortunately, this couple chooses to solve problems rather than be run by emotional conditioning. And their problems did become very difficult at times, almost getting to the point of their not wanting to sleep in the same bed.

It never got that far, however, because they had a prior agreement by which each abided. That commitment was—and still may be—that unless those Dresden dolls faced each other, they would not go to sleep at night until each one would be able to turn both dolls face to face. Of course, this meant that the two human beings would face each other and talk it out. Sometimes it might take most of the night and they wouldn't get to sleep until 4:00 a.m., but even though they had to arise at 7:00 a.m. in order to get to work on time, when they did awaken with the dolls facing each other, they also awakened with incredible energy. Each recognized that the thing going on in this world that was worth the most was the exchange of loving energy.

Again, this isn't a theoretical exchange of energy. I am talking about specifics. Sometimes a working person will come home with dirt on their shoes, leaving tracks on the floor. Their spouse may clean the floor afterward, understanding that dirt is okay and can be cleaned up, and sometimes the person will take off their shoes first.

There are more difficult conflicts, of course—those times when two approaches to an issue are seemingly incompatible and there doesn't seem to be a viable compromise or middle ground. Many people have divorced because of the inability to find a solution, while others have remained in a marriage of acrimony.

There is a third choice. You can take those things that are not working and actually move them outside the relationship. In a way, you put them in a museum. You can give each issue a name. In your imagination or in reality, if that's possible, you can take a photograph of it, a sculpture, or a symbolic piece of goods and put it in a glass case or in a cardboard box in the garage. You can write the name in a book that has a lock and key and put the book away.

The technique is for both of you to agree *not* to disagree; you both commit to making this a non-issue. You two make it not available for conflict by literally putting it away in storage, someplace that you both declare as off limits. As a result of this agreement, you never involve yourself in that "thing" in your relationship.

If you both go for this arrangement, it can have a remarkable bonding effect. As a result of your mutual agreement to "put it on the shelf" and to make it unavailable for conflicting approaches, you have made a commitment to solidify your living relationship with each other.

Will that issue ever be dealt with? Sometimes the issue will dissolve because of lack of energy. (When something isn't fed, it often fades away.) Then again, there are those "things" that can be kept "on the shelf" until there is a safe time and a safe place to deal with them. Don't be premature in taking them off the shelf. Make sure you both make an agreement (even if it's to keep it there for ten years) and stick to it.

The important thing about this technique is to keep the issue outside the relationship. That may seem to be a difficult concept to conceive, but if relationships were easy, you might not be reading this book.

Just for clarity, consider that there are many significant issues and events that are outside your relationship. For instance, there are satellites floating in outer space; there is a man fishing on a lake in the Soviet Union; there is a koala bear in a tree in Australia; there is night in another part of the world when you are having daytime. All of these things are outside your relationship, and there is nothing you can or should do about any of them. Put that seemingly unresolvable conflict with your mate at a similar distance.

Of course, your mind may tell you that it is not so, that the issue, the "thing," is right here and gnawing away at you. If you want a successful relationship, you might learn how to discipline the mind so that it holds a focus on what you want, rather than react to mental constructs that may not have much to do with your heart.

The likelihood is that if you have successfully kept your agreement to keep the "thing" locked away, and then you have dusted it off for review (at the given time you both agreed on—ten months, years, or . . .), the energy on it will no longer have a negative charge. In fact, it may actually have turned into a museum piece, a relic to view with interest as representative of another time long since gone.

What "thing" in your relationship consistently causes separation regardless of mutual attempts at solution? Only you can determine that. It may vary from expectations of physical proportions ("she's too fat"), attitudes toward relaxation time ("he only wants to go to the movies" or "she always wants to eat at the same restaurant"), or money, or anything else that you create as a conflict between the two of you.

Demands and expectations can lead to separation. If you both agree to put your demands in the museum, you are left with only acceptance and togetherness, which is the whole point of marriage anyhow.

Your mind may be arguing, "Doesn't putting it into a museum mean stuffing it? Doesn't the issue go into the unconscious whether you're dealing with it up front or not?" It doesn't matter where it goes. By putting your righteous (or "wrongteous") positions on the shelf, you are giving your heart the time to dissolve or resolve the conflict.

Some problems don't have to be solved by actions or words. Time will solve some problems in and of itself. This museum technique is calling on time and loving (which some people call Spirit) to resolve the differences you two may have created long before your conscious memories. It can happen if you are strong and loving enough to get out of the way and let Spirit work in Its own perfect timing.

Divorce in Love

Some people regard divorce as a terrible thing. It can be if the two people come from tradition, that place that gets into these kinds of conversations:

"You take the records. I'll take the books."

"No, I want the books."

"Okay, you take the books. I'll take the house, and you take the mortgage."

In that traditional place, a couple may spend their time fighting over material things. When they do that, loving can leave and anger can enter. Under those conditions, divorce can be a difficult thing.

There is another choice. Divorce can be a loving conclusion to a completed relationship. Yes, there might be some sadness involved, but it's not the kind that makes you want to hurt the other person. It's just a recognition that your expression with this person on the physical level is now complete. If the love between two people isn't working (meaning that it isn't creating more joy and abundance), then the relationship is probably over. If it is through, have the wit and courage to tell each other. It may be difficult if you view ending as a failure. Perhaps if you view the completion of your relationship more objectively, it may not be as difficult.

When people are more willing to be open and they refuse to live a life of quiet frustration, they may opt for divorce. They are more willing to say, "No, this is not working" and to be honest and clear, rather than live together in a marriage with truly irreconcilable differences. If loving cannot be found, it can be more devastating to stay together than to face the issue and know that divorce may be the higher choice.

It can be as simple as saying, "We've come to the end of what we can do together, and I want to be free to pursue my life in another way. But I don't think you're a personal failure or anything like that. I want to go because I've finished what I'm to do in this relationship."

Your partner may accede, or they may resist with, "What if I'm not finished?" You can ask, "How long do you think that would take? A few months, or minutes, or right now? Because, let's face it, together we just don't generate too much love. At best we're just tolerating each other. At worst we wait for a chance to get even."

The fact is, there is seldom a get–even status. One is always up, which means one is always down. If your being one–up is based on someone's being below you, you are as out of balance as the one below, maybe even more so.

Just because the physical relationship of living together is concluded, this does *not* have to mean that loving is ended. As a matter of fact, if you once truly loved your mate, even in divorce there is no reason for the loving to cease.

Some people who had a negative relationship while they were married can get divorced and, in time, can become friends. They can even get to be better friends than they were when they were married because they no longer place demands or expectations on the other, and what they're left with is an attitude of acceptance. That also means no judgment. Paradoxically, this is the perfect foundation for an intimate relationship. Too late, you may think. But it's not if they apply that attitude to future relationships.

Marriage, for better or worse, is a traditional choice that often works for worse rather than for better. Marriag-*ing*, a sharing of what is, with acceptance and loving, is an ongoing action that can be rich, rewarding, and one of the most deeply satisfying relationships you can have on this physical planet.

I encourage you to constantly make the choices that allow both you and your partner to win. That way, there is no better or worse. There just is.

2

Sex

Sexual intercourse is one of the ways the Soul involves itself with love on the physical level.

Sexual love exists when you love to have sex with a certain individual and share that particularly powerful energy. Within the appropriate framework, the sexual relationship is the highest physical form of union that a man and a woman can engage in together.

Individually, they can have other forms of spiritual union, but together, done in the right way, they can actually reach into a higher consciousness when this exchange of energy takes place.

Some couples have experienced this. Others have faked it. There is no faking out the truth teller that resides deep within you. No matter how good your act, that inner knower always knows. If you are willing to listen, you will hear the truth about your sexual expression. It probably isn't complicated. It may be as simple as "what will others think," that is, the god of opinion.

The truth teller within you knows whether or not the Soul is truly involved. It will let you know quickly and clearly about your sexual expression. How? If you haven't made love from that loving, caring place, within a short period of time after orgasm (or, in many cases, nonorgasm), the experience is over, *over and done with*. In those after–moments, there is often a sense of loss, a feeling of emptiness, a dull, unidentified ache. You can identify it as making love without the loving.

Men and women have often deprived themselves of an affectionate, physical expression of unconditional loving. Men have often forgotten that the woman they are with is not just a sex object but a love object who lives, breathes, cares, and feels. In that ignorance, men can deprive themselves and their partner of a sexual fulfillment that starts long before physical intercourse and lasts long after it is over.

Women, too, have often used sex as a negative expression instead of embracing the unconditional loving of the Soul in the physical form. Women have sometimes made love out of accommodation, expectation, and manipulation. They may have played at making love and faked passion, hoping to get a man's attention. They may have denied their love because of judgment or disagreement with the man.

Under the worst of circumstances, a man driven only by his lust says, "I love you" before the act, and a woman unsure of her participation says, "I love you" after the act. And it can all be an act. It may be valuable for you to realize that negativity expressed in sex (by omission or commission) will last long after the sex act is over. It would be to your great advantage if you would choose to treat yourself better. Why participate with such powerful energy in a way that is not supportive of your magnificent loving heart? The loneliness inside, after such an act, surely is not worth the price of a sexual expression without loving.

Doesn't it make sense to make love out of the affection of the heart rather than out of the lust of the groin or the fear of loneliness?

When Does Sex Begin and End?

The sexual act doesn't necessarily start in the bedroom. A couple can be talking over dinner in a restaurant, candlelight and all, and in their intimate sharing, sexual passions may be aroused. Your loved one may smile a certain way or close the blinds with a move that may turn you on. There may be talk about something of great interest, a powerful exchange of ideas, a personal sharing about something meaningful, or even a gesture of a single flower given with love. Any of these experiences may stimulate you sexually. Obviously, sex starts long before the explicit act of physical intercourse.

When was the last time you and your mate showered together? When was the last time you washed her back? Dried his feet? Rubbed his head when he was tired? Scratched her back until you eased that itch?

If you embrace everything you love about your mate while you are making love, there is no before-and-after. The entire expression is just one loving circle of lovemaking with no beginning or end. Know that you can also make love by kissing your mate very tenderly and saying, "I love you, my heart," and then snuggling and holding each other as you both safely fall asleep in the comfort of each other's loving.

Sex is the Soul making love in that tender moment of physical affection.

Sexual Information

We are living in an age of data availability, including sexual information. The good news about that is that we no longer have to live in the dark about sexual concerns. Men have found out that they most likely won't go blind if they masturbate, and women have found out that they won't be struck dead by lightning if they engage in sex before marriage. The bad news is that with all the information, the essence of the expression often is lost.

We have access to how-to books on sex, covering almost everything: clitoral and vaginal orgasms; the G-spot; premature ejaculations; impotence; techniques in touching, kissing, and positioning; the use of oils, salves, and aromas; and sexual aids varying from feathers to leathers. A lot of data. But does it matter?

The most important information is not technique, but that the sexual act is truly designed to be a *physical, affectionate expression of loving.*

Sex cannot be experienced from a textbook or consummated on a verbal concept. The sexual expression is one of the few things totally dependent upon experience. In the experience, you can simultaneously learn and pass the test if you are expressing yourself from your heart through all parts of your body.

There are great technical musicians, dancers, and singers who never reach stardom. Why? Because, as Louis Armstrong once said, "You gotta have soul." Satchmo had it, and so do Frank Sinatra, Fred Astaire, Ray Charles, Joan Sutherland, and Mikhail Baryshnikov.

The same thing applies as a lover. "You gotta have soul," and that is connecting to the universal Soul known as unconditional loving. That Soul is within you. To reach it, all you have to do is get your ego out of the way. You don't have to be the world's greatest lover (whatever that is). You don't have to be the most physically fit. You don't have to perform. You only have to *be.* If you and your partner accept each other as you are, in unconditional loving, then you will be the greatest—to each other. When love is expressed, there is no comparison.

You might be further ahead not to search out all the information available to improve yourself as a mechanical lover. For example, some books explain how to delay orgasm by imagining train wrecks. Do you know what happens when you participate in physical intercourse and delay your orgasm by envisioning a train wreck? You are dealing with a train wreck rather than your loved one.

You may know exactly how to move and to contract and expand your muscles just the way a book describes, but do you know what you could be relating to? A set of physical exercises. That may be more appropriate for an aerobics class than a lover's bed.

Is that what you really want? I doubt it. Almost every human being I know wants primarily one thing: to give and receive more loving. The sexual act is designed to be *a physical, affectionate expression of loving.*

Sexual Comparison

In this age of easy communication and permissiveness, we also have access to high–gloss magazines with low intent, along with hard–core pornographic books and X–rated video cassettes and movies. Of course, the models, actors, and actresses hired for such public performances will be generously endowed. Just as most standard Hollywood films employ people who are of extraordinary physical beauty, so, too, do pornographic film makers hire the exception rather than the norm (because all of the normal people would appear average in physical beauty and size; the uniqueness is the love and beauty inside).

What do the people appearing in sex magazines and films usually look like? They rarely have average bodies expressing sweet loving. The women appear to have 40–inch busts and 20–inch waists. They toss and moan in wild passion at the drop of a director's cue, "Action!" It is literally love *making*, otherwise known as acting, otherwise known as pretending. Playing their role in this pictorial fantasy are the men, who appear to have large sex organs and a staying power that would outlast a train.

Where does that leave you in relationship to them? If you buy into comparisons, you may feel as if you are less than zero. You might think there must be something wrong with you. You may think that you should get an implant, take a dozen vitamin E capsules a day, or see a therapist—anything but accept yourself as you are.

Some people may think, "How can I accept myself as I am? Did you see them? They're perfect and I'm zero." If you buy that image and compare, of course you can lose. That's the trap of comparisons. Even if you see someone that you think you are better than, you can be sure that someone better than you is around the corner of comparisons. If you compare yourself to a pornographic tale spun in a magazine or film whose intent is to falsely stimulate, you're likely to lose because you are real, and what you are reading or viewing is fictionalized reality.

There is a way to win, and that isn't by trying to fit any form out there. It is by accepting the unique, marvelous person you are, right here and now. Know that you are endowed with a physical body designed for you. Do you want to improve it? You can always exercise and eat proper foods.

But when you are in the middle of a sexual embrace with someone you love, you aren't in relationship to any of those externals. You are embracing the loving essence that just happens to come in the human form. At that time, the form you are embracing *is* perfect, as long as *loving* exists. When loving doesn't exist, no form is really perfect enough.

Another kind of comparison is envisioning or hallucinating someone, making them so real that you daydream the sexual act all by yourself. If you do this often enough, that hallucination may intrude while you are making love to your flesh–and–blood partner. You may not be making love with the real person, however, because the energy of the hallucinated figment of your imagination can come forward, thus robbing both of you of the loving exchange.

No matter whom you are sharing the sexual act with, you are never really having sex with anyone other than that one who is in your mind. If your bed partner is not your mental partner, then you are either with the wrong person or imagining the wrong person. Instead of living in your imagination and running a fantasy, you would be further ahead to be present in body, mind, and spirit with the person of your heart. Then when you make love to that special person, there is no fantasy intrusion because the reality is totally present and loving.

Is there a romantic ideal? There is, but it isn't a he or a she out there. The romantic ideal is a process, a we-process that involves considering the other person at the same time you are considering yourself. In fact, the highest romantic ideal is the process of sacrificing for the other person whom you love. Sacrifice what? Your ego, your attachments to a position, a physical possession, an opinion, and primarily to being "right." Sacrifice anything that stands in the way of your giving and receiving loving.

Is There a Gender Role?

Men are generally more mechanical than women. Their first sexual response is usually in the body. Women can be more sensitive in the Spirit. Their first sexual–type response is usually in the mind and the emotions.

If a woman feels that the man is being mechanical with her and not relating through the emotions, she might shut down physically. This might be caused by an unconscious reaction or a judgment of the man's behavior. In any case, this can leave the man frustrated and the woman separated. A more constructive choice might be for her to either relate to the man's level (not judged as bad, just seen as different) or bring the man into the emotional level.

The reverse has often happened, when the man has started to move into the spiritual awareness and the woman hasn't. Her unconscious response may be what some people refer to as frigid.

When both of you are relating through the spiritual expression, otherwise known as unconditional loving, the sexual relationship can be beautiful. Anything less may not support a balanced, nurturing relationship.

Years ago I was talking with a beautiful woman who was training me in terms of the woman's point of view regarding marriage counseling, and I asked her some questions: "How do you handle it when the husband wants to have sex, but the wife doesn't? Usually, you can't be as sexually lusting as a man because he's more often mechanical, and the woman is more compassionate and emotional."

"You're right," was her response.

"How do you get yourself up for his approach, then?"

"I am my husband's calm," she said. "Whenever he is upset, I can calm him down."

"What kind of upset?" I asked.

"It doesn't matter. Sexually upset, depressed, or anxious. He comes to me, and I am his calm. At an appropriate moment, we are both in sync, in loving, and then the mutual option is to make love because we're now a safe place for each other."

I was truly moved by their approach, but I still wanted to understand how they dealt with problems in their relationship (which didn't seem to be problems to them). So I asked, "What do you do when you're sexually aroused, and he doesn't want to be bothered?"

"He doesn't seem to know any better."

We both laughed, and I decided to talk to her husband and get his point of view. I asked him how he handled that aspect of his marriage. "When we first got married," he responded, "I was really interested in my wife in terms of my body."

"In other words," I asked, "you were sexy most of the time?"

"You got it. But I always knew there was also a depth of wisdom and something very tranquil about her. When I was with her, I was never as anxious to prove myself or release my body tensions as I had been with other people. We have this beautiful relationship, and she's always calm."

I felt like I was being set up. Although I met separately with each of them, it appeared as if they both had the same script. I asked him to clarify what he was talking about, so their relationship could be translated to accessible terms for us "normal" people who give, take, fight, argue, and love. He shared some more. "When a woman is supportively responding to you, she is concerned about your well–being and your happiness. She isn't just concerned about hers. It seems like she has given over."

I thought that was either a male chauvinist's fantasy or an incredibly ideal, unselfish sacrifice. I asked him, "What about the man's role in all of this?"

"When she gives herself over to me, there is no way that I am going to leave her unsatisfied and unhappy. I can't do that."

"What does that mean in terms of your sexual relationship?"

"Any– and everything," he said. "I respond in ways that I never thought possible. For her, I sacrifice all sorts of considerations to present to her something that is very special to me—and that is her. I sacrifice my considerations to present her to her through me."

I was beginning to get it, but I wanted to make sure, so I asked, "How do you do that?"

He responded, "She has a love with her. I take that love and present it through me. It is so pure that I want to give it back to her."

I heard the words, but I wanted to make sure I understood, so I asked, "How does that translate into your sexual relationship?"

He said, "I would enter into where she is, and I would become as one in and with her. I know exactly what pleases her. She seldom has to tell me or instruct me out loud, yet I know she is doing it in some other way. There is no way I can't be with her. That makes everything I do perfectly correct."

It became obvious to me that in their mutual sacrifice, they entered into the process of the romantic ideal. I asked, "What happens when human irritations come forward?"

"My irritations," he replied, "my urges, my upsets are usually all dispersed. I am in a state of niceness most of the time."

To me, it seemed as if the battery was charged and full, with no drain. His definition of their relationship said it all: "Together, we make the completeness of it."

Sexuality and the Creative Imagination

Many people are unaware that the source of the sexual expression and the source of the creative expression reside extremely close together within the physical body. There may have been times when you impulsively expressed sexually, when you may really have had a need to create something new out of your own beingness. If this has been so, the sense of satisfaction that came from sexual intercourse may have lasted only a short time, particularly in comparison to when you have expressed yourself creatively. The experience from the creative expression is a fulfilling process of longer endurance.

It is not the sexual drive per se that has the greatest influence on human beings. Rather, it is the imagination. The sexual act itself lasts a limited amount of time, whereas we usually spend much longer thinking about sex before the act. That is the power of the imagination.

The imaginative force is also a creative force. When you can harness it and focus your mind as you choose (instead of being driven by your sexual organs), then you are in charge of your destiny and creative life. This is not to suggest a renunciation of sex, or celibacy. It is another viewpoint, which may assist you in placing sex in a proper perspective for you and using it as an expression of fulfillment, as just one of many expressions afforded the body, mind, and emotions during this brief lifetime.

Sexuality and Spirituality

In its function, the sexual expression is a form of affection and creativity. The location of the creative urge toward sex and the location of the creativity of Spirit reside as an invisible band in and around the body, encircling the area just above the navel to about five or six inches below the buttocks (including the thighs).

Because of the closeness of the sexual drive and the creative drive of Spirit, people can practice spiritual deceit and become deceived. So-called spiritual people can become well-known as "bedroom athletes," which may be seen as an inappropriate way to use spiritual energy. This does not mean that the sexual relationship cannot be of a spiritual nature; it definitely can be an act of heightened spiritual exchange. Some people, however, seduce others in the name of spirituality; doing this puts them in opposition to the spirit of the occasion, and so the lessons await. In other words, all of us are under the law of cause and effect.

A relevant digression is an explanation of the psychic center called the "third eye," or "spiritual eye." Most people seem to think the third eye is located in the middle of the forehead, but actually it includes three areas: the physical area, the mental area, and the spiritual area.

The lower part of the spiritual eye is related to the physical level. People who have clairvoyant vision can see through the third eye and can use this ability to their own supposed advantage. They may try to seduce you sexually, in the name of spirituality, because they can see areas of sexual vulnerability and know how to capitalize on them.

The misuse or abuse of sexual energies can lead an individual into conflict with the religious or spiritual law, a situation not easily resolvable. The way to ensure that you don't create conflict with these laws is to be honest. If you are expressing lust, call it lust, instead of telling someone, "I love you," and five minutes after the act wishing you were alone. If you say your sexual expression is spiritual and it's not, you may be committing a "spiritual crime."

There is no way to escape the repercussions of a violation of these laws, but because they must be fulfilled, you carry the balancing action within you. You are the judge, jury, and executioner in carrying out the sentence of the law. (And, eventually, you will discover the fullness of God in you, too, which is the source of total love and forgiveness.)

When people feel the energy of Spirit, they may misinterpret it as a sexual desire. Although misinterpreting is easy and tempting, there are ways to work with these situations.

The spiritual thrust is up and out; the movement of energy is up through the body and out the crown of the head. The sexual drive releases through the reproductive areas. If the spiritual energy is released through the sexual act (particularly through sexual intercourse that is lacking in loving), it can become negative creativity. It can be like an anchor holding you to your created limitations on this physical plane.

When the sexual drive builds within you, you always have the option of bringing that energy up through the body. You can feel the energy being released through the top of the head instead of through the lower centers. The most supportive choice is to express and release the energies in integrity, with a partner in loving and/or into the higher levels of Spirit. Whatever you do, the choice is always yours, and so are the results.

Sexual Fulfillment—Releasing Negativity

Much of the fulfillment of the sexual act comes as a result of the balancing of the positive and negative polarities of the man and woman. The man has a greater positive polarity in his body, and the woman has a greater negative polarity in her body. This does not relate to good and bad; it's simply opposite polarities, as in a battery, both of which are essential to making things work.

At the time of sexual intercourse, there is an electro-magnetic chemical charge that takes place between the man and the woman. This charge is what produces sensation. It's vital. It makes the battery glow and the energy flow.

The man releases his negativity into the woman during sexual intercourse. The woman receives of the negativity

and then releases it during her menstrual period. It is during this period that the woman releases that which was given to her and that which will not bring forward new life.

Women

In most so-called primitive societies, a woman has her menstrual period as easily as washing her face, but in our "civilized" society, we have made a natural process much more difficult than it has to be.

Most women in the Western culture have learned at an early age that childbirth is purportedly an agonizing experience. Some see films depicting this, and others read articles or are told by others that it is horrible. The young girl who gets this fearful information will probably have an instinctive, protective reaction of "I'm not going to do that. It's too painful!"

Then, because we are all powerful "creators," she may create a forceful resistance to the whole process. A few years later, when she starts her menstrual period—which represents the potential of childbirth—she may get cramps through the abdominal area and lower back every month. That girl, who has been programmed to fear childbirth, may now have a difficult time releasing the negativity during the menstrual cycle.

When a woman has a history of blocking her creative flow and shutting off this area of expression by pushing the energy back down into the creative center, she may develop many problems related to her menstrual flow. She may release her negativity partially through the altered glandular functions of her body. At times, she may also feel grave anxiety and apprehension and may express in sudden spurts of anger or impatience, feeling better after she has released this way.

51

It is obviously more difficult to release negativity when the normal channels are unavailable. Yet it is interesting to note that when a woman is in the positive, creative process of childbearing, she does not have her menstrual period.

Both men and women can express resistance and stubbornness at times. Women who experience those traits with regard to the creative process can also find themselves with weight problems. As they express resistance, they push energy into the lower centers of creativity and reproduction. As the energy is pushed into this area, it attracts excess weight there (the area from just below the rib cage to the upper thighs). Women often gain weight just before their period and feel bloated and uncomfortable. This is often because the resistance pattern has increased the irritation and negativity at this time.

It can be difficult for a woman to lose weight held in the body through the pattern of resistance. Diet can help, but a change in attitude can help even more. If the attitude can become one of acceptance, release, and flow, the weight can drop off and the cramps may taper off.

Problems such as cramps, lower back pain, weight gain, false pregnancies, and even hysterectomies can be lessened or eliminated by a positive attitude of acceptance toward the body and its natural functions. Just knowing these things and working to change the expression to a more positive one can assist tremendously. The first law of Spirit—acceptance—is also the first law of the physical body.

Men

Men who do not release their negativity through the process of energy exchange with a woman may release it in other ways. They may have a lot of nervous energy and may produce a great deal of action but very few results.

Masturbation can be another release for a man. The power behind masturbation is a little less in the sensation of penis stimulation and more in his mental imagery, his fantasy of what he would do with his penis if the person were present. The energy released through masturbation goes toward the picture he has created. Although the picture may fade as the man subsequently involves himself in something else, the essence of the influence stays with the creator, resurfacing later in his consciousness. Then he is most likely to masturbate again. If the man does that enough times, he may become hooked on that fantasy type of expression. As a result, a man (either single or married) who masturbates a great deal may have sex not with a woman as she is, but rather may cast her as part of the imaginative act in his fantasy.

When a married man or woman secretly masturbates, the other person may think their partner is not interested in sex (because they already had an orgasm). Some men will intentionally masturbate before having sex with a woman so they can be a "great lover" and not have an orgasm for a very long time. The only difficulty is that a man who does this may not be having a loving sexual relationship with his partner. Instead, he may be a performer having sex with himself because his partner is just a participatory audience.

There is a way to transmute those energies and get rid of those sticky fantasies that attach themselves to the creator. It's a matter of rising above their energy field and dissolving them. One process that works is called spiritual exercises.

Spiritual exercises are true magic—not illusion or sleight of hand, but an expression that can change and erase negative energies and pictures that may have been hounding a person. If a person stays down with the negative images, in the lust, they cannot transmute them, and the person may be run by their creation.

At some point in a person's life, a choice can be made to say "pass" to the influence of negative fantasies. Those who choose to rise above the negativity and gift themselves with the power of the higher realms through spiritual exercises are, indeed, giving themselves the gifts of freedom.

Men (and some women, too) may also release negativity through drug or alcohol abuse. These expressions may release some negative energy, but they are also likely to create other problems for the man, indicating that these forms of release are not the most constructive or desirable. Men who block the flow of their creative energy may develop prostate gland difficulties and other problems related to the genital area.

As I have said, the creative and sexual centers reside very close together in and around the body. At times, you may experience the stirring of creativity by Spirit, and this may simultaneously stir the sensual part of the sexual organs. Then you may move to the fantasy or reality of a sexual experience. So, what is originally a spiritually creative experience is interpreted as the desire for sex, and you may then act upon that desire. Most times, under those circumstances, you won't feel fulfilled. You may be left with that empty feeling, knowing something is not quite right.

How do you learn the difference between creative and sexual urges? When you get what seems to be a sexual urge, you could express creatively and/or spiritually, letting the sexual expression be put "on hold" for a while. In time, you will be able to differentiate between the close but different urges, and you will express yourself in ways that are most beneficial to your wellness and balance.

When the sexual drive is thwarted or is producing guilt or dissatisfaction, it may move into the stomach and intestinal areas and the shoulder, neck, and facial areas.

Muscle spasms can occur, the face may break out in rashes, and parts of the neck may swell and become painful.

When some couples have sexual intercourse, the husband is not a lover, but a machine, and he may complete his mechanical action before the wife. Then she may feel resentful, or she may complete the action by herself, possibly experiencing guilt and confusion because she believed the sexual act should be one of mutual, uplifting togetherness. The vision of togetherness is only possible if two people are willing to deal with it, honestly and without ego.

The man must be smart enough to learn to love the woman he loves as she needs to be loved in order to be satisfied. It is important that he talk to his lover and clear things so this can happen.

During sexual intercourse, two people come together in the closest relationship possible on the physical level, and they owe it to themselves and each other to come together with as much love, understanding, consideration, and freedom as possible, so that they can make the sexual expression a joyous and fulfilling experience for both of them.

Sexual Attitudes

People have been conditioned to relate to sex from different points of view. Some regard it as necessary, in order to make babies. Others complain of a headache in order to avoid sex—and not just women, either. Some men, too, have become complacent, too tired, and occasionally bored, particularly in a lengthy marriage.

Some women go through with the sexual act because of their expectations about the marital relationship, but not with joy. They reluctantly receive their husband's body without really giving of their own. Some men do not approach the sexual act with consideration, care, affection, and sensuality. Some men regard the act only as one of relief, and they behave accordingly.

Some people regard parts of their bodies as off limits: "No touching or kissing there! You better not do that! That really turns me off." That "that" which you say turns you off may be the result of a judgment that you learned before you were an adult. That attitude has nothing to do with the passion and loving expressed in the sexual act.

You have probably read enough books and magazine articles and seen enough pictures and movies to know about some of the variant expressions within the sexual act, whether it's this position or that, whether it's oral or physical intercourse or the many different expressions of the sexual act.

If you have any no's or refusals regarding the sexual expression, you might want to look at them and make sure you aren't saying no to the loving. Of course, I am not saying that you shouldn't have choices and preferences in this area. If some expressions cause you physical discomfort, it is certainly your option not to participate. If they cause you discomfort because of cultural conditioning, however, you might want to look at the situation. You may be imitating someone else's experience that has little to do with your own loving, spontaneous sexual expression. You may be reflecting such limiting attitudes as, "Oh, a real lady wouldn't do that!" "I just can't let the father (or the mother) of my child do that to me!" "That's disgusting!"

What is disgusting to some may be the only way to others. If you limit yourself with cultural, societal, parental, or gender conditioning, your relationship may also be limited. With loving, you can go beyond such conditioning from the past and express freely in a direct, spontaneous, present-day relationship to your lover.

The sexual act need not come through past conditioning, and it need not come through mental judgments or your ego. The sexual act does need to come through your heart. Then the rest of your body follows, from the tip of your head to the toes on your feet and everything in between.

Giving of yourself and receiving your partner can be a joyous freedom—not necessarily those ways shown in books or films, but those ways that spontaneously erupt while you are expressing love.

Express and experience sexual love as if your partner is the most precious being on the planet. And if they're not, what are you doing with them?

Is There a Sexual Morality?

There is a sexual morality created by human beings, which is specific to gender, nation, mores, culture, and an era. In the United States during the 1930s and 1940s, the attitude toward sex was the double standard: "Good girls don't do it until they're married," while there was an unspoken attitude permitting the men to do it before marriage, "but not with a woman you respect." After World War II, sexual attitudes evolved to greater permissiveness, tolerance, and expression, as birth control became more widely used and economic conditions improved, making divorce less punitive. All these factors influenced attitudes toward the sexual expression.

Then came the 1960s and 1970s, a period of profound cultural and political movement in the United States. With assassinations, a war in Viet Nam, an explosion of drug availability and usage, and the birth control pill, the pendulum swung away from the double standard toward total so-called freedom. (I say "so-called" because freedom without responsibility often gives birth to anarchy rather than joy.) In the eighties, the pendulum has begun to swing back. After the promiscuity of the last two decades, men and women have begun to realize the greater value of sex as a rare and particular expression, an experience of loving rather than lust. Perhaps this recognition is timely because the 1980s also brought forward—through sex— highly contagious diseases, such as herpes and other more fatal diseases.

Many men are no longer the male predator seeking sexual conquests. Many are easing off promiscuous sex and beginning to realize that the sexual act is not one to boast about, but one to share on a more profound basis.

Women, who had been at the distant end of a double standard, found their sexual expression during the 1960s and 1970s to be permitted with much less stigma. In the mid-eighties, they seemed to be moving toward the more poignant position that to make love casually is less than fulfilling. For the first time in decades, some women (and men) are embracing a form of abstinence and celibacy, not as a restriction, but as a positive expression. And when they do choose to make love, it is often a more profound expression.

Once chosen, the sexual expression itself has no intrinsic restrictions, although it is often influenced by cultural, gender, and individual standards, which change with the times. There are many different ways to express sexuality, and none is necessarily good or bad. In Spirit, there seems to be no morality, no right or wrong ways to express sexuality. Morality is an aspect of society; men and women decide their own morality, which varies according to culture, age, gender, and time in history.

At this particular time, we are more aware of bipolarity, of a person's carrying a balance of both feminine and masculine energy. This androgynous consciousness is awakening in many. People with this consciousness may or may not feel an urge to express sexually. They may not need the sexual expression since they already possess a form of balance of both positive and negative energies. Yet they may express sexually as fulfillment on an emotional level, and they may marry and have families in a comfortable, loving expression.

Some people with an androgynous consciousness may express in a heterosexual, homosexual, or bisexual manner. Within the range of possible sexual expressions, they have many possibilities. They also have the choice of maintaining their own creative–energy balance, using the energy to lift themselves into higher levels of consciousness. A person of predominantly male or female polarity also has this choice, but the androgynous person will usually find this easier to do, particularly when they understand and learn to work with their own nature.

Are there sexual variants or deviants? I prefer not to label or judge anyone, although there are, of course, such classical categories as voyeurs, nymphomaniacs, those involved with fetishes, transvestites, hermaphrodites, transsexuals, and so on. And there are homosexuals and heterosexuals.

I do not support anyone's imposing their sexual preference on another. Spiritually, however, there seems to be no morality in these areas. It is primarily through negativity that we have placed moral judgments on these expressions. It's similar to young people being told that if they touch their reproductive area, they'll go crazy or blind.

When you get high enough above the negative levels of the body, you can have intelligent liberation *now*. In this intelligence, you can enjoy the lower levels with less chance of getting caught up in them. That still does not give you license. You need to be judicious about your sexual expressions if you don't want to create imbalances that you will eventually have to clean up.

In the Soul, there is no indication of morality. There is just the purity of the essence of God. In that essence there is no morality. There just is.

No-Goal Sex

I suggest you don't get locked into the traditional gender roles of the woman receiving and the man giving. That can be beautiful, positive, and very loving. The reverse can also be true; it can be just as beautiful and positive in any given moment as long as loving is going on. There is a feminine part in the man, which is capable of receiving, and a masculine part in the woman, which is capable of giving. Don't cast yourself in any role except that which spontaneously arises.

Be in the present. That means that you don't caress or express only to achieve a future state, result, or effect. Don't bother with ratings (leave that to television shows). Don't bother to keep track of the number of orgasms, how long you lasted, the last time you made love, or any other record keeping. Be a lover rather than a bookkeeper.

Express yourself with every part of your body *from your loving heart* as you are at the particular time. If a particular gesture pleases you, you can express in sound and movement a reaction of a desire for more, different, or whatever, as long as you are responding in the here and now.

What happens in terms of quality and quantity of expression will occur of its own loving accord. If you focus all your conscious energy into a desired result projected into the future, you may deprive each of you of the extreme loving pleasure of the moment.

The sexual expression can be different each time. If you try to repeat last night's success, you may be experiencing tonight's failure. When the sexual expression comes from the loving heart through the body as an expression of now and now and now, any– and everything can be part of the success approach.

People express in many ways during the sexual act. Some cry in loving, laugh in loving, observe in loving, assert in loving, are passive in loving, are receptive in loving, are primal and animalistic in loving, are downright silly and funny in loving. Any of it can work if the source is *loving*.

A long time ago I bought my dear mother a beautiful set of chinaware, which was very expensive. She loved the set and said, "I'll save this for special occasions." I didn't care for that, and I said, "I got this for you and Dad to eat on all the time. You two *are* a special occasion."

The same thing applies to you and your beloved partner. You two *are* special, and every time you make love *is a special occasion*. That doesn't mean that you can't be spontaneous; I encourage that. When loving is involved, the more in the here and now you can be, the more alive the sexual expression can be for each of you.

Sometimes the man may be assertive; sometimes the woman may be assertive. Sometimes you may make love in a bed; sometimes, on a rug. There are times you may make love for an hour; other times may be for 20 minutes. Some people prefer to make love during the night; others, in the morning. What matters is that you make love in loving.

Be in relationship to that unique person you and your partner are. Give to and receive from each other as if it is the first time because, actually, each time is the first time as long as you express the love existing inside of you at the moment.

Sex, God, and Ego

Love is of God. When we are relating to the things and people around us with care and consideration, we are infused with God's love and joy. When we are not handling things in that manner, our awareness of God's ever-present loving energy may be blocked by such lack of caring. It's almost as if we have created a situation in which God does not cast pearls before swine. In that sty of negativity, not-caring often manifests as judgments heaped on others. This can be particularly evident in the intimate expressions that take place in bed.

Part of intimacy in bed (besides sexual intercourse) is sleeping together, something people often take for granted. Actually, sleeping together is a very intimate, trusting experience, although we have sometimes abused that intimate comfort.

How many times have you been in bed, stewing with anger because you knew the person next to you was "wrong" but wouldn't admit it? What did that get you except righteous indignation, as you kept company with a bad taste in your mouth, a dry throat, and a tense stomach? You could have bypassed that righteous indignation.

Your response might be, "I tried. I mean, if she'd only admit she was wrong, everything would be okay." To that, I'd say, "I'm not talking about trying that way. That's just perpetuating the judgment."

Another response might be, "If he'd stop being so pompous and arrogant, I'd let him in." I would say, "That's not in; that's out in the judgment jail you put him in. There are other ways, if you're willing to bypass your ego."

"Such as?"

"When your lover is lying there in bed, just gently pull back the sheets, sit at the foot of the bed, and massage the bottom of the feet. As you do that, you can say something to the effect of, 'I don't like being separate from you. I don't care any longer about who's right or wrong. All I know is that I love and care for you, and please forgive me.' "

To this suggestion, the person could respond in the traditional way with, "I should ask her to forgive *me?* She's the one who's wrong!" Another person might similarly answer, "Rub his feet? After what he said to me?" The best thing those people might do is send the ego, with its lack of awareness, out for a walk.

Be careful of sticking to your guns because you might then get locked into the destiny of a gunslinger, and, believe me, there will always be another relationship waiting around the corner for you to gun down or to gun you down at the not–OK corral.

If you want to live with someone in warm, loving, caring, caressing support, I suggest you bypass the ego and go for that tender moment. You know your partner better than I do. Does he like his temples rubbed? Does she like her back massaged—you know the place, in the back behind the heart?

I know a couple who kept each other's skin clear. To some people that may sound gross, but to that particular couple, they are like loving monkeys, cleaning each other and calming each other in the physical–bonding process.

Whatever gives sensory pleasure is the place you can touch with the energy of loving. When you do, you two may end up making sexual love, or you may not. It doesn't matter because what is being expressed is loving. If you lean over and gently kiss your love and say, "Good night, my beloved," that loving can blossom by morning.

When loving is involved, sex, God, and you may all be one.

3

Children

Children are truly God's loving creations. When they are born, they come onto this planet with a mission of learning how to give and receive love unconditionally. Unfortunately, some adults forget this and sometimes relate to children as if they are deaf and dumb slaves with no intelligence, sensitivity, or feelings. I've heard too many adults say "shut up" to a child rather than "I love you." I've observed more adults tell a child, "Just sit there and don't say anything," instead of listening to the child's point of view. I've heard adults say, "Do this," and when the child asks for a reason ("Why?"), I've heard the adult say, "Because I said so!"

Often, because the adults are not in touch with their own loving, they may have difficulty expressing loving to children. Perhaps, too, these adults were not shown caring and consideration when they were children. The cycle of pain and ignorance can be perpetuated, from generation to generation, as the actions of the parents are placed upon the children.

Some of the first conscious recollections of children are often negative directions: "Don't do this. No, not that." Parents may sometimes find it easier to negate children than affirm them and are sometimes quicker to say no than yes. They can be more prone to be impatient and critical than to accept and say, "Do it as well as you can." They may sometimes find it easier to focus on what is wrong than to say, "How good you're doing that!"

Out of a sense of responsibility, parents may tend to take over and manipulate the consciousness of the child. For example, almost every parent has, at some time or other, insisted that the youngster eat everything on his plate whether the child likes it or not. The parent has probably not realized that children often know whether the food is proper for their nutritional pattern. Babies are sometimes finely tuned in to their bodily functions and needs.

It takes an open, alert parent to receive the child's messages, particularly since the child is not communicating in a language adults understand. Make no mistake about it, however: infants do have a rapid, lasered form of communication. They receive and send on levels adults may have long since forgotten.

I know of one infant who was totally tuned in to her parents' emotional states. For example, when the mother was irritable from a phone conversation with a close relative, the sleeping infant, in a bedroom on the other side of the house, would wake up and cry. The crying was in empathy for her mother's upset.

I know another four–month–old baby whose father had to take a job out of town and returned home only on weekends. On the first night of his return, the baby woke up crying every ten minutes. The mother was exhausted from caring for the infant all day and needed sleep. The father understood and, in his loving, moved a thick quilt next to the baby's crib and slept on it. Every time the infant awakened, the father would mumble, "It's all right, baby, I'm here." There was empathetic communication between the two, and eventually they all slept well. The important thing is that they woke up in loving togetherness, complete as a family unit.

I know of one particular parent who did respect the baby's inner knowing when she refused to eat any baby food for the first ten months of her life. Although the parents were concerned, one of them somehow tuned in: "Look, she's healthy. She doesn't get sick. She's happy. So what if all she wants is milk. She'll tell us when she's ready to eat anything else."

They tuned in and respected the child's awareness. That baby grew up to be a healthy, vibrant, energetic young lady. Many parents, however, take their responsibility and the child's lack of adult communication as authorization to manipulate and control, particularly the child's eating habits.

A parent may issue the edict, "Now, eat everything! I want to see a clean plate before you leave the table." Those children who obeyed because they feared disapproval may have forced themselves to eat it all, and this eating habit sometimes became an ingrained form of getting approval. The unconscious of the child took care of its responsibility to clean up everything on the plate. This programming may go with the child into adulthood, and the adult may continue to eat everything on the plate. Out of fear of losing love and approval, an obedient child can become a corpulent adult.

If a youngster doesn't perform according to the parents' standards, the parents often give impressions of withdrawing their love. By pretending to be taking their love from the child, the parents exercise control, demanding that the child perform according to the parents' desires in order to receive love. That is emotional blackmail, which can be disastrous programming to a child who is supposedly loved.

If you wish your children to grow and prosper as constructive, loving human beings, I suggest that you do not teach them that form of manipulation. One of the last things you want them to learn is that this technique—of giving and then taking back love—is a worthy device. To do this could, once again, be a case of the ignorance of the parents being visited upon the children.

My definition of sin is just a matter of missing the mark, of acting in ignorance. You have the opportunity to increase your awareness and, thus, bring an end to the ignorant behavior of previous generations. It starts with you as an individual. You can treat your child with the loving care, dignity, respect, and concern that you want for yourself.

Children are total human beings. They just happen to be smaller and have less physical experience on this planet–Earth level. Not dumber, just less experienced. Do you remember the first time you drove a car that required manual shifting? The car may have sputtered with jerky movements because you gave it too much gas or too little gas; the engine died, and you almost caused an accident when you tried to park backing up. That wasn't because you were dumber than your instructor. You just had less experience.

Your relationship with your child can be even more loving if you consider the possibility that you and your child have contracted for a relatively brief relationship of instructor and student. (Not judge, jury, and executioner.) You can be a loving, patient instructor to the student/child (and sometimes you may also be the student to your teacher/child).

There are circus trainers who teach wild lions and tigers with affection and rewards, and the animals respond beautifully. I think our children deserve at least the same treatment. The result would most likely be a joyous relationship in which both parent and child gain.

Be a Consistent Parent

I am *not* suggesting that out of your love, you allow your children to have or do anything they want. That isn't really love; that can be more like laziness and indulgence. An important part of loving is to establish guidelines and help your children stick to them.

We need to work with children according to their levels of perception. As adult to adult, we can be flexible and change our minds and attitudes toward many things, many times. While an adult can accept, tolerate, and even adjust, a child has a more limited perception.

I knew a mother who did not relate to her child in a very consistent way. Instead, her tolerance varied widely. At one moment she was easygoing, and the next she had a hair-trigger temper and was indignant. For example, when her boy watched television, she would call, "Dinner is ready." He'd respond, "In a minute, as soon as the commercial comes on." She'd wait a minute or two and then call, "Come on. Dinner's on the table." He'd call back, "Just a minute, until the next commercial comes on." She'd be understanding, chuckle, and go in lovingly, pick him up, kiss him, and say, "Come on, now, honey," and take him to the table.

The next night she called, "Come and eat." He responded, "Just a minute." This time, however, she went in, grabbed him by the ear, forced him into the kitchen, forced him down in his seat, and yelled, "How many times do I have to tell you?"

The child never knew which way his mother would respond. One night the mother made it fine for him to delay coming to the table, and the next night he had no breathing room.

This mother did not work with the child according to *his* level of consciousness. Parents need to do that if they want to help their children move forward in growth, understanding, and responsibility within their own plan and destiny.

Your children do have their own path in life, which may be entirely different from yours. You can let that be okay and can support your children in their learning. One of the ways you can do that is by setting and then sticking to consistent and loving guidelines.

Being a Perfect Parent

Children often feel the most insecure with an adult when they don't know if they're going to get kicked or kissed. That's because we, as adults, often vacillate: "To vacillate or not to vacillate; that is the question. Isn't it?" We are often inconsistent inside ourselves. *Inside ourselves,* for it all starts inside. Our outward behavior is just a reflection of our inner balance or out of balance.

Look at yourself as a parent. Are you usually very consistent with your child? Or are there a fair number of days when you are unhappy with your adult life and let that affect how you relate to your child?

How about those times when the washing machine breaks down, the water from the refrigerator has seeped through the linoleum, and you get a telephone bill for calls you never made? Do you get irritable and take it out on everyone in sight, including your child?

How about when you come home from work ready to quit the job because your boss is behaving totally unreasonably and you are faced with bills that make you aware of how much you need to keep that job? Do you ignore everyone, including your child?

Even though your child didn't cause any disharmony, he is being treated as part of the problem.

When you are upset by something, you don't have to try to behave as if nothing is wrong. You can admit to your child that you are going through something. You can share on a simple level, saying that you have certain problems to solve. It will be much better for you and the child if you are honest on the level the child can understand. You don't have to share all of your trials and tribulations, but you can be a human being with normal frailties rather than parade yourself as perfect.

You can easily say, "I'm trying to work out something, darling, and it has nothing to do with you. I just need some alone-time." It might be a lot better for the child (and for you) if you shared honestly. Isn't it possible for you to say, "Honey, I'm a little off today, so please understand that I love you even if I may be a little impatient." The child may not understand all the words, but he will get the sharing on a level that's important. When you share your own human frailty, your child also gets that it is okay for him not to be "perfect," also.

Of course, there are always some parents who come from an authoritative, righteous position. Their attitude says, "I am perfect and you, my child, are always imperfectly messing up." The fact is, however, that parents aren't perfect, and neither are children. They are teaching each other the lessons necessary to grow. If you are involved in anger, frustration, or any emotional extreme, there may be less room for growth because progress and growth flourish in an ambience of loving.

How do you relate to your children on a day-to-day basis? Do you use TV as a baby-sitter and send them to watch television rather than play with them? And then do you yell at them when they're watching TV, "It's ten o'clock, get to bed, move it"? The children then run off to bed alone, possibly feeling as if they did something wrong because a parent has yelled at them in that impatient, something–is–wrong–with–you tone of voice.

That may get your children to bed, but not in a loving consciousness. One of the most important times for children is right before they go to sleep. Others are the mornings when they awaken and their mealtimes. If you just make the effort to express loving consideration during those periods, you will be doing much to support the growth of a loving human being.

Take that opportunity of walking your child to bed, tucking her under the covers, and spending some time talking, as a loving privilege for both of you. That's a revolutionary idea for some parents. "Talk to my child! About what?"

How about, "What did you do today that you'd like to do tomorrow?" Or "What is it that you did today that you don't want to do tomorrow?" If you ask those questions with love and interest, your child's answers may surprise and delight you. This loving process can also assist your child in letting go of any disturbances of the day, setting up a clean slate for a positive experience tomorrow.

What do you say when your child says, "I don't want to go to sleep?" Some parents treat their child like that mute slave and shout, "I don't want to hear it. Go to bed and be quiet!" There's another choice, however. You can tell your child, "Oh, you don't have to go to sleep. I just said it's time for you to go to *bed*. That's a special time when you can be by yourself and make up stories and songs and draw pictures, all in your mind. It's a private world in your bed. In the warmth of your bed during the dark, you can create a marvelous place."

In other words, you don't have to be punitive or demanding. You can assist your child by presenting the required behavior as a positive, particularly privileged experience. The same thing applies to cleanliness, home-work, and all those other things that children don't usually do easily. Support them in the positive options, instead of taking a berating, insistent attitude.

Part of loving is to create an atmosphere of freedom and to teach the child that with freedom comes responsibility. Part of loving is also to provide the child with what is needed to develop her own loving heart. Sometimes that is called discipline, which may produce the freedom to be more loving in a happy household. Good habits can be taught, and loving choices can be encouraged.

How do you teach and encourage? Words can help, but they aren't the primary teaching tool. Love is the greatest instructor. I know someone who loves to cook and who has a loving experience while cooking and serving. There is a tangible, delicious difference between this person's food and the food I prepare myself. That's because I don't love preparing food as much as this person does. Even if it's just breakfast cereal and milk, when this person serves it, the loving energy makes a specific difference. (I don't have sensitive taste buds.)

The same thing exists when "cooking" for a child. If you enter the experience with a loving joy, the information will taste so much better and will be more easily digested by the child.

Of course, this is a generalization, and as with most generalizations, it will work as you work it. There will be times when the less–than–human condition raises its frail head, and you and the child express impatience. That's all okay as long as you make it okay. You can give yourself and your child leeway to go through the ups and downs of the learning process. Your child is just beginning to grow and learn, and, believe it or not, you are not finished with your learning, either. You can learn on both the outer and inner levels throughout your life. Since you are the more experienced one, you are in charge for a short time—in charge of directing, stimulating, encouraging, urging, disciplining, and, at all times, loving your child.

Yes, there will be times when the child will push your patience, but it won't be pushed to the maximum because the fact is that your loving can provide as much patience as is necessary each time. Remember that part of loving is sometimes saying no. I am not advocating permissiveness under the guise of loving. I am advocating loving under the guise of loving. I am advocating the point of view that your child can be a source of fun for you, not a trial. Your child can be a help, a joy, and an inspiration, as you can be to your child.

When you don't have to, don't be in charge. If the child is hiding under the blankets and you say, "Come out, come out, wherever you are," and the child doesn't come out, you can still talk, touch, and laugh through the blanket. As long as it does not endanger the child or break an arrangement on which you two agreed, give your children freedom to express themselves even when their expression is different from yours.

There will probably be many times when you ask your children to do something and they make it clear that your idea is not their choice. If you start to get impatient or irritable, you might ask yourself this question: "Do I want my children to do this because of my will or ego, or because it's necessary?" Some parents have complained, "My kid goes through periods when he doesn't want to talk. He's sullen and just wants to be alone." Isn't that all right? Haven't you had periods like that? Remember, children are human beings, only smaller in size and somewhat limited in physical experience.

If what your child is doing (or not doing) may cause physical harm to himself or others, of course it is your responsibility to help avoid that in the best and fastest way you can figure out. If your children ignore an agreement, it is also your responsibility to remind them to keep it. Teach the value of sticking to the guidelines, or negotiate new ones. If you are unwilling to do that, your child may grow up to be an adult who has no respect for adult guidelines, including the law.

An English theater critic once said, "Theater should be run by a committee of three, two of whom are always absent." This is similar to a household with parents and children. Everyone has an opinion and a point of view and should have the right to express that, regardless of age or status. Yet, when it comes to voting, implementing, and enforcing the decisions, there is a situation of "two of whom are always absent." In this case, the adult, the parent, is the one in charge who has the vote. (I once heard a teenager object to that and call his father a dictator. The father smiled and said, "Yes, but a benevolent dictator.")

It isn't a matter of democratic majority rule in a household. It's not that I'm for discriminating against younger people; I just know that, generally speaking, someone with 34 years experience on this planet has much more information on which to base a decision than someone with only 14 years. Of course, there are exceptions, such as when a 17-year-old might be wiser than a 42-year-old ("and a little child shall lead them"), but, for the most part, I am talking about the average family situation.

This child-raising process will almost surely test you, the parent. Your patience will be stretched and your imagination called upon. Perhaps there will be those times that you choose to go along with the child (even when their request *seems* incorrect) for the sole purpose of their learning a lesson, as long as there is no danger or harm involved.

At the same time, don't make it a federal crime if a child messes up. If the child makes errors, in school or at home, understand that making errors is part of learning. If a child were born perfect, you wouldn't be needed. Let the child know that it is okay to make errors, from missing a question on a test to spilling the milk. If you make it all right to do well *and* to make mistakes, your child will probably not lie to you. How marvelous to have a parent–child relationship where neither one lies.

"Oh, I never lie," some parents may say. But what about when the child had a splinter and asked if it would hurt to take it out? Many parents lied to their child and said, "No, not at all." They could have told the child the truth: "Sure, it will hurt a little bit, but a lot less than if we let the splinter remain and infect your toe."

Even with sensitive issues, such as sex, I urge you not to fabricate to "protect the child." Our children have been too exposed through television, movies, and music to resort to "the birds and the bees" or a perfunctory "good girls wait till they're married." Tell the truth as you perceive it, and share the values that you have experienced as beneficial. (The key word here is *experienced.*)

The optimum choice is to tell the truth or—if the occasion demands it—to say, "I'm not ready to share all of the information with you," or words to that effect. It's all right to tell a child, "This is a little too complex for you to understand now. In a little while, we can sit down and really talk about it."

If you develop the habit of telling your child the truth no matter what, your child is likely to treat you the same way.

Raising a child isn't always easy, but it can be easier than we often make it. If you relate to your child with loving consideration and respect, when that child gets to be 16, you probably won't have a problem on your hands. You're going to have a friend who will be a joy and comfort.

On the way, during this growth process, remember to touch. That's right, touch. A hug, a pat, a squeeze, a stroke—all those loving, physical expressions are recorded in the child's heart forever. Reach out and place that loving energy in the sensory heart-bank of your child's life experience.

It is important to give your child direction. Children need direction. Because they don't always know that, they may sometimes push, pull, cajole, and lie to get out of adult direction. When they know they can't get away with it, however, they will actually be grateful and cooperative— perhaps reluctantly at first, but eventually with total willingness. If you vacillate when the child is very young and don't hold to your word (regarding promises, rewards, and requirements), you will probably have greater difficulty when the child becomes a teenager.

In loving, use the spirit of correction with youngsters because they may involve themselves in the spirit of manipulation. Love them and yourself enough not to put up with anything less than the truth—from yourself and from them. They may not like it initially, but in time they will respect your allegiance to the truth.

Children may sometimes see your holding to truth as punishment. Eventually, however, as you stick to the truth guideline, they may reluctantly accept it because you give little choice in the matter. Eventually, they are likely to embrace the truth standard as the only way to go, all because you held steady in your loving awareness and insisted that truth be part of the family relationship between you and your child.

Teens: The In-Betweeners

I have heard parents bemoan their experiences with their children, whom they described as going through the "terrible teens." This may often be a difficult period for your children as well as for you. Your teenager is actually in between being a child and an adult. They get confusing messages from both the adult world and the children's world.

For example, when a parent or teacher is upset over a teen's behavior, they often say to the teen, "Grow up. You're old enough to know better." When a teen does something that the parent or teacher disapproves of, they may say, "Don't try to be such a bigshot. You're still a kid."

Teens get demands and responsibilities put upon them as if they were adults, and that contributes to their growth. They get restrictions and guidelines as if they were still children, and that contributes to their growth, too. This situation, of course, can also contribute to confusion.

In this confusion, teenagers often form that private club where adults have no entry. The private club usually manifests in an assertive hands–off attitude toward adults. Teens will dress and arrange their hair, makeup, and jewelry in ways that many adults find strange, weird, or even repugnant. Some adults think that teens are destroying, or at least distorting, their physical beauty when they change styles to suit their generation. From skinheads to punks, from long hair to mohawks and to things we haven't imagined yet—our children will do them, to be sure. They will ensure the private teens–only club by inventing their own language, for which an adult often requires a translator.

Parents can take a number of different attitudes toward this, not all of them necessarily constructive. If your ego and a need to control your child are involved, both of you may be in for difficulties. You may force your child to dress or comb their hair the conventional way of your generation, but, in doing this, you may also plant a powerful seed of resentment and rebellion that can manifest a lot more seriously in years to come.

Another option is to be more of an observer. As long as

your teen child/adult is doing no physical harm to himself/ herself or anyone else, you may as well see the humor in it and know that this, too, shall pass. In case you don't think so, just remind yourself of when you were a teen and re- call your dress and attitudes toward your peers, parents, and the entire adult world. Today's teen rebels may be to- morrow's responsible citizens. If their behavior does not harm themselves or anyone else, I suggest you permit that expression and even enjoy it, as strange as that might seem to you.

There are other expressions, however, that may be harmful. Some teenagers are heavily into drugs and alco- hol. These illusion-producing chemicals can do severe harm to physical, emotional, and mental functions. Drugs can definitely impede growth, learning, and spiritual devel- opment. I suggest that your attitude not be that of a judge and jury ready to sentence your child to a life of no parental loving, but rather one of corrective guidance.

It's most important to keep the loving and acceptance going. Understand that it is possible your child may try drugs or alcohol. If this happens, don't come from shock, outrage, or an I-told-you-so position, especially if you used drugs way back when or if you need that drink to relax when you come home. Do come from compassion, under- stand peer pressure, and share your point of view. Share objective information on the effects of drugs and alcohol. Share from your positive point of view, emphasizing your child's natural value and how your son or daughter may be harmed by drug and alcohol use.

I shared this point of view with an acquaintance, who responded, "Suppose I do that, and my kid still takes drugs. In fact, I think he got high right in my own living room. It sure smelled like it. How do I deal with that?"

My response was, "Just remind yourself of your posi- tion and relationship. Be the 'benevolent dictator.' You are the boss of the house, if you claim it."

"Yes, but I've told my son about the harmful effects of drugs dozens of times, and he still uses them. What more can I do?"

"What privileges do you give him now?"

"None, really. I mean, he's 16. A kid 16 is mostly on his own."

"Do you pay the rent or the mortgage?"

"Sure, of course."

"Then let him know that if he doesn't live by your rules—no drugs or alcohol—he can't live in the house for which you are paying the bills."

"I can't kick my son out of the house!"

"All right, do you feed him?"

"Of course. I don't want my son to starve."

"Then let him know that if he continues to take drugs, you will no longer provide food."

"But he'll get sick if he doesn't eat properly."

"And he won't get sick indulging in drugs and alcohol? Do you give him any spending money or lend him the car?"

"Yes, he has an allowance and a driver's license. When I'm not using the car, I let him borrow it."

"How about cutting out his allowance and keeping him from using the car?"

"That's pretty drastic, don't you think?"

"Don't you think using drugs is drastic? Don't you think that during his precious teen years, he deserves to have a clear mind?"

"Actually, they're just recreational drugs. I'd be a hypocrite if I didn't admit taking the same drugs many years ago. I mean, he's not involved in the hard stuff. Besides, he only uses them when he's upset. To relax, he says."

"It sounds like you're justifying his using drugs."

"No, not at all. I just don't. . . ."

"Don't what?"

"I don't know what to do."

"Sure you do. But maybe you're just not willing to do what it takes to actually do it. Sometimes you have to be willing to be the 'bad guy' in order to get your son to be good to himself."

Do you, the reader-parent, see yourself in this conversation? If you do, you don't need to judge yourself. Instead, you can recognize the value of the information and realize that you can take steps to support your child and yourself.

There is an old saying, "Nobody cares how much you know until they know how much you care." If you are willing to put yourself on the line and make and uphold unpopular decisions in order that your children live in reality rather than drug-inspired illusion, you must then give them direction. You must give your children guidelines. If they resist, you can impose these guidelines as long as they live in your house, as long as you are paying the bills for their food and upkeep, and as long as you love them enough to dare to care.

This is not to imply that you will deny your children their experiences of learning. You are part of their experience, and so are your guidelines. That doesn't mean you have to be so rigid that your child can never make a mistake. Growth usually comes through making mistakes and then learning from those mistakes. Your role as a parent is to do all you can to ensure that your children have the opportunity to learn rather than repeat the mistakes. You'll know they have learned when their behavior has changed.

Be a Responsible Caretaker

Just because you are a father, this does not mean you

are a *father.* A biological father is a sperm donor. Just because you are a mother, this does not mean you are a *mother.* A biological mother is an egg bearer. It takes a great deal more to be a *mother* or *father* in the sense of nurturing, caring, and taking loving responsibility.

We have to realize that we are caretakers, which is our real responsibility to our children. One of the most difficult tasks for a parent is to become a neutral caretaker and to establish guidelines for the child's growth in learning, love, and safety, without suffocating their individuality. Many parents can become attached to certain behavior, making it a demand, and they often approach the child emotionally.

Your child comes into this world ignorant of how to function successfully here. Your first job is to train your child to behave as a socially appropriate human being. Initially, it's quite elementary. You train the child to follow simple commands, and thus she learns the language. If you are to be a truly good parent, you will also exemplify the model for her to follow. I know it's sometimes easier to give lip service to the way you want your child to behave, and it can be a matter of "don't do as I do; do as I say."

Being a role model for your child means that you accept mature responsibility for your own behavior while you remember that you, too, are still learning (although children, of course, generally relate to their parents as all-knowing and all-finished in that learning process). Do you and your spouse fight? Do you argue loudly? Do you get into disagreements with fervent emotional outbursts? Do you do any of this *in front of your child?*

If you want to teach your loved child to grow up to be a loving human being, one of the worst role models you can provide is the omnipotent parents fighting with each other and expressing out-of-control emotions. Your behavior—that which you demonstrate in front of your child—is one of

the greatest teaching devices, and the greater your awareness, the more likely it is that your child's lessons will be
more positive than negative.

So many adults think their children hear or see only
when they are directly addressed. I have heard parents say
outrageous things in front of their child, but because they
didn't talk directly to the child, they assumed the youngster
wasn't receiving what they said. Don't deceive yourself as a
parent. Know that your children, *from the moment they are
born,* are receivers. (There is even evidence that children are
aware of the outside environment before they are born.)
With all their senses, they get what is going on, even if they
remain in silence. So be aware, and choose what you want
your children to get and not get.

I am not saying that adults shouldn't disagree, be
emotional, or fight. That is also part of the human process,
although I do know that part of the human process is also to
transcend the emotional hurting (but that's for another
chapter). If you are going to have an argument with your
spouse, make sure you do it at such a place, time, and
decibel level that your children do not see or hear the conflict. Such battles are your adult lessons and are not to be
imposed on the children. And don't assume that because
the children are sleeping, they don't hear your raised
voices. If they would be able to hear your voices if they were
awake, they may also receive the discordant frequencies
while sleeping.

When children know that the parents have highly emotional disagreements, they are likely to exploit this adult
separation. It's the old gambit of saying to one parent,
"Dad, can I have the car? Mom says I can if it's okay with
you." Then, of course, the kid goes to the mother and says,
"Dad says I can have the car if it's okay with you." Be
vigilant in the face of the child's Mom–says–Dad–says ploy.

An easy way to handle this is to make sure you and your spouse are both in the same room when the child makes his or her play.

Part of being a responsible caretaker is keeping your word in both positive and negative situations. Don't promise your children that you'll go to a school play they're in and then not show up. Don't threaten them with a punishment and not carry it out. Don't even threaten them with such expressions as "I'll skin you alive" or "I'll brain you." While those expressions seem impossible, they may register on the child's consciousness. Certainly, the emotional energy behind such words will impact, and although you may subsequently get the child's obedience, you may not realize the emotional cost.

Tell your children exactly what you want them to do, in simplistic language: "I want you to wash the dishes. I want you to dry the dishes and place them in the cupboard."

Of course, there will be occasions when the child breaks a dish or knocks over a glass of milk for the third time, spilling it all over the freshly laundered tablecloth. Make sure that in your reaction, you do not value the dish or tablecloth more than your child. Breaking, falling, scraping knees, and dropping things are all part of the process of learning. Do what is necessary to help your child become consciously aware and to concentrate and avoid accidents, but also let there be room for mistakes, without their becoming major catastrophes.

Just understand that the process of growing up never ends. Even you, I hope, are still involved in that process— which reminds me of a saying: "It's never too late to have a happy childhood."

Bonding

Bonding is a primal act that involves touching. It is a physical expression of caring and nurturing, a tactile way of saying, "We are one." Some people think that bonding occurs only among animals, such as chimpanzees. We human beings sometimes forget that we, too, are part of the "animal kingdom."

Children, particularly infants, need bonding. A baby will often cease crying when held or just touched, calmed by the loving energy of the parent that is transmitted through the physical connection.

We have all known our children to lean on us, hang on to us, assume almost any kind of posture just to make sure that their bodies are touching ours, regardless of what we are doing. That is a primal instinct in the child, who is acting out of the need to connect with the parent's loving energy.

The most profound bonding (for both the infant and the mother) may be when the mother nurses the child, but bonding can occur without nursing and isn't restricted to gender. One father I knew would go into his crying infant's room and just rub his finger gently up and down her back, and she would stop crying. A mother would carry her child on her hip with one hand for hours at a time, while she did most of the household chores (cooking, putting the diapers into the washing machine, even running the vacuum cleaner). Another father used to walk up and down his baby's room, holding the child against his heartbeat, and a mother would hold her baby in her arms, as she rocked for hours.

When bonding doesn't occur, the child may get sick, unconsciously creating an illness in order to be touched. During an illness, the parents will often soothe their child's forehead, rub the child's little back, and do other things that involve physical touch.

Don't avoid touching; embrace it. Skin to skin is most effective when loving is transmitted. You don't have to concentrate or focus on it. It's just a matter of doing it. Regularly hugging with affection, holding hands, gently massaging the neck and shoulders, taking a bath with your baby, having your child lie on your chest or belly—they're all expressions that contribute to the physical, mental, and emotional health of the child and the parents.

Bonding is important not only between parents and children. It is also extremely important for adults to touch—not just as a sexual act, but as an expression of loving, caring, and sharing. The form of the touching doesn't matter as long as it's loving. Some couples give and receive back rubs, manicures, or hair brushing; anything is fine as long as there is caring in the touching.

Bonding with your child is also a simple and effective way of "making up." Parents sometimes lose their temper and yell at their child; quite often it is programming they picked up from their own parents, another case of the ignorance of the parents being visited upon the children. If you become aware that you have done this, the best thing to do may be to just pick up and hold your child. Then get a drink of water, and both of you sip, for the cleansing and the love. When you discipline your child because it is necessary for the child's learning, bonding is also valuable. When you touch and hold, even in the middle of discipline, your child will understand that within the discipline is love. Under any anger or frustration you might express, caring can also be communicated by bonding.

As children grow older, their peers often become more important than their father and mother, and if bonding didn't take place between the parents and their child, the parents are often greatly distanced by the child. You can help avoid that situation by bonding with your children when they are young. It doesn't have to be a big production. Bonding can occur through many small acts. Sometimes ten seconds of a loving touch will do it. You can pick up your child, hold her securely, and let her experience your loving. The form doesn't matter. It can be a hug and a kiss. It can be with fingertips. It can be throwing the child in the air, catching her, and enveloping her in your hugging arms. These physical expressions of love make you a father, make you a mother, far beyond the biological definition.

Do you want your child to grow up to be a nurturing, caring, supportive human being? Children learn by imitation. If you participate—often—in such bonding acts with your child, the odds are that by the time your child is a young adult, you will have contributed to this world by bringing forward a positive human being radiating great warmth and loving.

Wise couples often manage to get away from their children. This is not a crass, selfish action when it comes from an awareness of the adults' need to have time alone. The parents need to be alone with each other, without concern that a child will interrupt them. They need to renew their adult bonding with each other, independent of the child.

Your child can be one of the most important people in your world (and despite rumors to the contrary, children are people). Make sure, however, that neither of you parents makes the child more important than each other because, in time, the child will mature and leave you two alone together. If you have not already secured your adult relationship, it may be less than stable without the child.

Unfortunately, too many adults have repressed their expression of touching. Too many people have grown to think that the need to reach out and connect physically—not sexually—is less than mature. Bonding isn't a matter of maturity. It's a form of transmitting loving energy through a physical connection.

First-Child, Middle-Child, Youngest-Child Syndrome

Some parents have said that insecurity in a particular child resulted from that youngster's being a "middle child." Others have blamed insecurity in another child on her being the youngest and, therefore, receiving the least amount of attention and needing to compete with her older siblings. Other parents have told me that their first born was the most insecure because he had to give up his parents' total attention and share it with the brothers and sisters who came after him. I suggest that parents of more than one child don't fall as easily into that trap.

Insecurity can come to a child occupying any position in the family. The way to deal with your child's insecurity is not to label it "middle child," but to address yourself to the insecurity. It is the child's self-image that is the real issue, not the position of the child on the family tree.

The way to build a child's self-esteem is to pay specific attention to what the child says and does. If she gets good grades or her teacher says something nice about her, write it on a piece of paper and put it on the bulletin board. Or if the child made a particularly beautiful drawing (children's drawings are often full of wonder, or wonderful), frame it and hang it.

Don't make monuments to what the child does poorly. Those are just learning patterns. Instead, affirm the successes so the child will grow with success, not failure, as a frame of reference.

If you are a parent with more than one child, make sure you arrange time with each one, individually. For example, on alternate evenings, you can take a short, quality walk with each—alone—and have a sharing that is attuned to that particular child. Almost anything you and one of your children do together will give the message that the child is more than just one of "the kids" and is a valued and special individual.

If you want to build your child's security base, do not compare his performance with that of his brother or sister. Each child is born with individual patterns that involve past, present, and potential. Appreciate the fact that each child moves at his or her own rate of progress. (Incidentally, so does each parent.) One parent I know, who has three children, is aware of this. Sometimes, for example, he throws one child up in the air, and with the other kids, when it's their turn, he does a different kind of physical play.

A mother I know encouraged her three children to study musical instruments, but the guidelines were that each child had to choose a different instrument. Therefore, there was no direct competition.

You can look at first, middle, and youngest children from a traditionally limiting point of view and, perhaps, contribute to that limitation unconsciously. Or you can change your attitude, and instead of looking at each child's position in the family from a limiting perspective, perhaps you can see it in a more positive light. For example, the first child can be seen as the "miracle child," the one the parents stare at in awe, viewing each expression as miraculous. The first child often gets the fresh burst of the parents' loving and all their attention.

The second, or middle, child is the one who gets the benefit of his parents' knowledge, since the parents already have experience. The second child also gets an instant companion in having an older brother or sister, and if he happens to have a younger sibling, he has the opportunity of learning how to handle things faster on his own and how to take care of someone (like his younger brother) and develop nurturing qualities.

The third child, let's say the "baby of the family," can get a special kind of attention and loving from the parents and support, fun, and loving from his older siblings. He may also have an easier time when he is a teen because his older brothers and sisters *may* have paved the way for him.

It's all a matter of attitude. There are many ways to help build your children's self-esteem through support and a positive attitude. It can be as simple as picking up one of the children and saying, "Come and look at the sunset with me." Then both of you go outside and share the glory of nature—just you and that child.

The next evening you may say to that child, "Remember the sunset we saw together?" And, of course, the child probably will. Then perhaps you can say, "I'm going to take out your sister and look at today's sunset with her, okay?" Most likely the child will respond positively, and that is just one of the many ways you can bond with your children and help build their self-esteem.

One single experience won't necessarily build a child's self-esteem immediately. Particularly with children, repetition and long-term consistency are necessary. It also doesn't have to be a sunset, of course. It can be combing a child's hair or gently rubbing the child's head while he or she lies in your lap.

As part of your helping to build self-esteem in the different children, I suggest that you do not give the children hand-me-down clothing if at all possible. Family finances sometimes make that necessary; if that is the case, perhaps you can make a special effort to make that hand-me-down different and to let the child know it. For instance, you can tell the child, "This was your brother's shirt, but he's outgrown it, and it is just your size. But you're different from your brother. How can we make this shirt work for you? Should we dye it, or sew something on it, or put a patch on it?" That child is likely to respond positively to these kinds of caring actions, especially if you make sure that each child (regardless of age, position, or size) does get *new* clothing occasionally. When a youngster does get new clothing, you might let the older child give the new clothing to the younger one, thus permitting them to bond through the clothing. Then when the older child gets something new, the younger one can also feel good about it, because now each has had that experience.

Single Parent

Single parents are no longer an obscure minority. There are so many single parents now that they are almost as much a part of the mainstream community as traditional married couples.

Most single parents are women, mothers. That is both the good news and the bad news. The good news is that the mother, who carried the child during gestation, is also likely to have the endurance and nurturing qualities necessary to be a loving role model for the child. The bad news is that the single mother cannot provide something that is of great benefit to the child, male polarity and guidance.

This is not really news, because single mothers are generally aware of the need for a male role model for the children. Perhaps the impulse of providing the maximum for their children may contribute to a woman's search for another mate. While I appreciate that quest, I suggest that women not get married just to get a father for the children. Get married for the love of one adult for another adult. Within that, the love of children can be expressed and even learned.

Part of the difficulty in maintaining balance as a single parent has to do with the parent's meeting his or her own needs, which are often different from those of the child. Adult companionship, nurturing, romance, sexual expression, and playtime are all valid yearnings.

Many of our needs, legitimate as they may be, are sometimes difficult to fulfill, and with single parents, there can be an additional complication. Their adult needs may often come in direct conflict with the needs of the child, on the physical, emotional, mental, and spiritual levels.

Since the overwhelming majority of single parents are women, I will be addressing women here. Understand, however, that most of what you read can also apply to the single father.

I have spoken with and counseled many women in this paradoxical situation, women who needed male companionship as a normal, healthy expression. Some women have not permitted a man to come to their home, even when they were going out on a date. As one mother expressed it, "I don't know if I even like the guy enough to spend more than an occasional night on the town with him. I'd rather not have my impressionable daughter get confused about another man. What I mean is, she might get more attached to him than I do, and if I decided not to see him again, she might go through a feeling of separation and loss, on a smaller scale but similar to what she felt when her daddy left. So I meet my dates in the restaurant."

Then there is the opposite point of view, as expressed by another woman: "One of the primary rules I have for me and my children is that we never keep things from each other or lie to each other. So if I'm going through an investigation of relationships, it's fine for my children to be aware of it. I don't want my children growing up in a fake Mommy-and-everything-else-is-perfect world and then to be shocked by the traumas of reality when they are grown. So, sure, I have men pick me up and drop me off at the house. Later, when I'm alone with my kids, they ask me how I enjoyed myself, and I tell them the truth. Sometimes it was boring. Other times, great."

I'm sure there are many more attitudes that cover the spectrum of choices. It is not an easy situation, particularly when, as a single person, you might want to express yourself sexually. Then very real concerns come up, such as, "Do I go to his place and then leave because the baby-sitter has to be home by 11 o'clock?" "Do I bring him home and go to my bedroom and just hope the kids don't awaken?" "I don't want the kids to get the impression that maybe he's their next father, when, actually, I just needed to be held for a night. So, do I kick him out in the middle of the night because I don't want us all to have breakfast together?"

None of the choices is optimal. Subjectively, however, I'd suggest that single mothers and fathers use care and caution before exposing their children to their dates. Children endow their parents with a kind of omnipotence, a wisdom and a knowing; although we know that parents are only humans and are learning, making mistakes, and correcting themselves, a child does not yet know that. Your children will watch whom you date. Because they love you and endow you with omnipotence, they will unconsciously assume that the man you are dating is your wise choice, although that date may be just part of your own adult search for a person with whom to share love. Sometimes we are less than wise in our choices, and that, too, is our learning experience, but it would be better if our children did not have to endure some of the negative side effects of our adult experiences.

I do not have specific suggestions about how the single parent can pursue her adult needs (in primary relationships, financial matters, jobs, etc.) when they appear to be in conflict with the child's needs; the options vary, depending upon specific circumstances. I do know that it is incumbent upon the parent to recognize that giving birth to that child was her choice and with that choice comes responsibility. The responsibility is sometimes inspiring, joyous, and deeply meaningful. We also know that raising a child can bring everything from fulfillment to boredom, from being a loving support to being a maid, from rapture to the ridiculous. That's all part of the deal.

There will be times when the other parent's presence is truly missed, by both you and your child. There is a comfort when disciplining, for example, if the mother can sometimes resort to that old line, "Your father will deal with it when he comes home." The mother, who often has the long-term endurance, can sometimes use the immediate impact of the father in disciplining a child. Also, at the end of the day, when the mother has been involved in everything from baby talk to baby's diapers, she often needs another adult to share with on an adult level. It is those end-of-the-day hours that can sometimes get difficult, for both you and your child.

It is during these times that I suggest you do what you can to support yourself, within the responsibilities that come with being a single parent. This can vary, depending upon your needs and choices. Some adults can get lost in a book and get the away-time they need. Others need to talk with an adult friend, perhaps during a late afternoon walk in the park or on the telephone. You may create some sweet ritual that you establish with your child as "quiet time," with each of you doing a separate thing and making no noise, which leaves you to your own thoughts, meanderings, daydreaming, meditations, or spiritual exercises. Sometimes 15 to 20 minutes of that can be as refreshing as a cool shower on a hot day (which is also another choice).

One of the most important things to remember is not to judge yourself if and when you need a break, relief from the day-to-day tedium of handling responsibility for your child. You can love your children and still need time to be alone or just with other adults. Experiment with positive expressions, finding that which lets off steam without emotion, that which permits relaxation without false inducement (drugs, alcohol, or tobacco). You can form a community of friends who have similar concerns so that each of you may support the others. It isn't always easy, but it is always worth it. If you have any doubts, just watch your child while coloring or daydreaming or even one night while he or she is sleeping, and you'll know that your choice of bringing that child onto this planet was a noble one.

Bringing forth that Soul to awaken during this life is a responsibility the parent can willingly embrace or feel stuck with. It's a matter of attitude because, no matter the choice, you still have the responsibility. In accepting responsibility, you may be called on to make sacrifices. Rather than resent the sacrifices, perhaps you can look at the rewards that come with parenthood. I don't know anything more creative than nurturing another human being. The adage "as you give, so shall you receive" is never better exemplified than in a giving parent and a loving child, a mutual gift to each other.

As you bring up your child, with all the challenges you may encounter as a single parent, I suggest you remind yourself that you are entrusted with that being you often call "my little angel." He or she is not only *your* little angel but also *God's* little angel. You can love your angel and teach your angel, and you can even make mistakes with your little angel. Just know that you, too, at one time were someone's "little angel." Perhaps now, though, with your greater knowledge, you can do a little bit better with your "angel" than your parents did with you. It's not that they didn't love you enough. It may just have been a matter of their not knowing enough to do better. As you learn and become more aware, of course, you will be able to do better—for yourself and for your children.

At those times when life's sandpapering gets rough, be it your finances, job, or relationship with another adult, your child will be part of that experience (even if it's on the unconscious level). Don't judge or punish yourself for the conflicts, the struggles, or the errors. They are part of life. If you approach each experience with integrity and with loving care for your child and for yourself, that's the best you can do. Your child, too, will learn that conflicts can be faced and handled, particularly when there is loving.

Role Models for Children of a Single Parent

Most single mothers are concerned about having a role model for their children, particularly their sons. If the mother has been divorced or separated from the biological father and is still feeling hurt because of conflicts with her ex-husband, this may cloud her ability to evaluate him as a role model for her son.

I encourage both parents not to let emotional distress lead them to deal with the other in ways that separate and confuse the children. Despite any problems you and your "ex" have had, it would assist you to recognize that God is in your child and in the child's father and in the child's mother. As you remind yourself that it would be good for all of you if you come from your heart and not your emotions, you may be able to clean up things and balance issues with your ex-husband or ex-wife. Even if the issues between you and your former spouse may not be resolved, you can always say, "Lord, please give him (or her) the love I could not give." Then you can let the acrimonious separation go.

To be redundant—and repetition is a major form of teaching your child (and the child within you)—it is for your advancement and, certainly, for your child's advancement for you and your former spouse to transcend your emotional reactions to each other and place your child's welfare first.

If each parent is responsible and loving, I suggest you both support the child's spending time with the other parent. In cases where the parent, the father, for example, is not an appropriate role model (e.g., he is involved with drug or alcohol abuse or other inappropriate behavior), then someone else may be in order. Sometimes this can be a relative, a best friend, or even a neighbor. Sometimes boys will also find positive role models in books. These can be heroes from Hercules to Jesus to Moses or adventuresome characters who overcame adversity, such as those written about by Jack London. Regardless of the choice, the mother can encourage her son to identify with the person or character: "There is something about you that reminds me of him."

Throughout childhood, your children will be faced with tests, trials, and tribulations, which can be stepping-stones in their growth, and I suggest you let them learn from their experiences. Every parent naturally wants less pain and more success for their children, and you can do all you can to create an ambience and attitude that lead your children toward positive experiences. Know, however, that scraped knees (physical and metaphorical) are part of the lessons bringing growth. Let your children have those opportunities, and support them as they learn.

The best way you can support a child is through awareness, loving, repetition, and bonding. As many times as it takes, as many touches, as many words, as many hugs, it will be worth it because you are involved in one of the most creative acts possible on Earth. You are contributing to the positive growth of a loving human being.

Children and Religion

Many parents (single and married) follow the religious experiences of their parents, and they often pass on those attitudes and beliefs to their children. Sometimes that is positive; at other times, it can be a case of religion by rote. For example, some parents insist that their children attend religious school or say their prayers every night according to the words passed down by their parents. Religion learned by rote and enforcement seldom awakens the individual's heart to the love of God.

Many people pay homage to God only on a word level, with just their lips, not their hearts. Others may focus on the "thou shalt nots," evoking a powerful, punishing fear of God. If that's what you want for yourself and your child, that's your choice.

Another choice, however, is to love God and to awaken to God's love for each of us. I prefer the perspective that we human beings are God's beloved creation, moving from imperfection into greater spiritual awareness and at–one–ment with God.

Regarding our children, I would much rather share my joy in loving acts, as expressions of Spirit, than *demand* similar behavior from our youngsters. We can best teach our children about God by loving them with the love of God. I am not concerned whether a child (or anyone) is involved in the same spiritual group as I. I don't care if a child chooses to be a Baptist, a Catholic, a Mormon, a Jew, a Buddhist, or a participant in the Movement of Spiritual Inner Awareness. I do care that a child understands that he or she is loved by God and is encouraged in those things that strengthen such knowledge.

When I was a child, my mother used to sing a song to me that said, "Jesus wants me for a sunbeam." I thought that was terrific at the time. Then one day I became aware of what a sunbeam actually was: you could see dust floating on a sunbeam, and a sunbeam would show the dirt on the windowpane. I decided I didn't want to be that. I'd rather be a young boy who could be Jesus' friend. Some parents might find such an attitude too independent for a youngster. Fortunately, my mother didn't, and, as a result, my love for Jesus is based on another experience, rather than the words of a song.

For the sake of your honest relationship with your children, my suggestion is that you not tell them about the benefits of a spiritual expression unless you have experienced it yourself. Most children have a subtle truth barometer inside them that knows when you are telling the truth based on your experience or when you are talking from a concept of expectations that is more theory than practice. If you lie to your child (by omission or commission), your youngster may be less likely to tell you the truth. (This includes occasions when your child may observe you lying to someone else.) Conversely, if you are honest with your child, your child is likely to return that honesty. And that is one beautiful experience.

My father told me that kids are to be spoiled. I believed that. Spoil your children with love, care for them, and let them know they are really accepted into this world as they are: dear human beings who have much to learn.

Everything you offer your youngsters should be for their learning and upliftment. Everything. All the time, even times when you are saying, "Be quiet." Rather than punish or berate your son when he doesn't respond immediately, you can be creative: "Let's see who can be quiet the longest." Then set the timer, as you *both* find the joy in being quiet. Or you can show your daughter that being quiet isn't negative, as you take her to the window and look out, contemplating the world, in silence, together.

Then they learn quiet. And if you do it right, they learn that you love them. Is there a greater learning than that?

4

Communication

We cannot have a relationship without some kind of communication. In order to ensure that we are all sharing the same language, allow me to communicate *Webster's Collegiate Dictionary*'s definition of the word *communicate:*

1. share
2. to convey knowledge of or information about
3. to open into each other
4. to reveal by clear signs
5. to transmit information, thought, or feeling so that it is received or understood.

Despite the above definitions, *essence* is seldom communicated. Most of the time, people will communicate from their egos, emotions, desires, expectations, or yearnings.

How do we get to a place where communication is a process of sharing information that is not distorted? Perhaps we might initially run the assumption that we are going to communicate to someone who is a valuable, worthwhile human being.

Of course, this might not work unless the communication is also *from* a worthwhile, valuable human being. If you do not regard yourself as such, you may start to communicate facades, distortions, judgments, or lies.

So, you see, in order to communicate, you must first accept yourself as you are and as good enough just as you are. Every human being—*every person alive*—is truly a valuable, worthwhile being. It would be to your benefit to remind yourself of that, particularly during emotional times when the information you are communicating may be colored by your conditioned needs. Remind yourself that the person to whom you are talking is a valuable, worthwhile human being (even if they aren't behaving the way you might wish).

Because people often place things in the way of essence communication, it would be valuable for you to take the time and make the effort to create an environment that permits any level of communication from others. I have been in amusement park fun-houses where there was what might be called the "crazy room," a room where the walls and floors were made with such material that people could jump, fall, leap, walk, or crawl—and no one would get hurt. Imagine a place where you could not hurt yourself or anyone else (not such a crazy room, after all). Some imaginative, aware people engineered this safe space.

In your relationships, you can become a safe-space engineer. You can design a space—inside of you—where you cannot hurt yourself or anyone else, particularly those participating in your daily life: your wife, husband, child, lover, boss, colleague, companion, teacher, automobile mechanic, accountant, and, certainly, your parents. In a safe-space environment, no matter what differences occur, information can be communicated with no recriminations, guilt, fear, or punishment.

Communicate What?

Most positive forms of communication have a subtext of wanting to give and get more love, care, and abundance. Think about it. Even many political, ecological, social, and

economic concepts have an undercurrent of wanting to create conditions wherein loving thrives, and they often deal
with the desire to create more loving in tangible forms. The
difficulty comes because people differ on the forms of expression. Some think they must exclude others in order to
gain abundance for themselves and for their particular gender, ethnic group, country, or religious sect. They have not
yet realized that unconditional loving is the highest communication available. An unlimited supply exists, not only
in theory but, when the consciousness is awakened, in the
pragmatic political, social, and economic areas, too.

If I want more joy, that's for my own gain. One of the
ways I get more joy is to share it with you. It's a living
paradox. The more I give away, the more I get. Yet there
are those who operate from another point of view: "I'm
going to have joy at your expense." There is little value in
that type of communication. Who wants to be around communication forms that hurt?

The Declaration of Independence of the United States
affirms that "all men are created equal," and that includes
both men and women. It can't mean that people are physically equal because, obviously, we are not. Some are
stronger, weaker, taller, shorter, fatter, and thinner. It can't
mean equal in talent because we are not all Mozarts, Stevie
Wonders, Joan Sutherlands, or Magic Johnsons. It may
mean equal in opportunity, although in economic and educational areas, even that isn't entirely true. Then equal in
what? *Equal in the capacity to love?*

I have seen a little girl being hugged by her father.
There was no issue of whether they were rich, poor, black,
white, thin, or fat; the level of loving present is what
counted. I have seen couples marry in Africa, China,
the United States, Mexico, England, Egypt, Israel, India,
and the Canary Islands. The capacity for loving in each of

those brides and grooms is equal. A primary thing that
can detract from the equality of loving is lack of essence
communication, essence meaning the heart-level caring
and sharing.

The Subtle Traps of Communication

In this age of growing awareness, consciousness raising, and sensitivity, many individuals and couples involve
themselves in a committed effort to communicate—with
themselves and their partners. The avowed purpose of this
commitment is to share, to clear up misunderstandings,
and to move toward greater intimacy, support, and loving.
Many times, this works beautifully. Within this, however,
there can be subtle traps involved in communicating feelings, hurts, or blame, and the expression that started out as
a movement toward greater intimacy can sometimes result
in separation and acrimony.

Why does this happen, since the individuals usually
are well-motivated and want the same thing, that is, more
loving and greater intimacy?

An illustration of this was apparent when I counseled a
couple. The husband started by saying that he was interested in having a closer relationship with his wife. He felt
that the closeness that had existed during the early days of
their marriage had dissipated. Because fear is one of the
greatest blocks to true communication, I asked the man
what his fears were. He responded that he was afraid of the
commitment. He was fearful that this particular relationship might not be *the* one for the rest of his life. As a result,
we discovered that he had been undermining and sabotag-
ing the relationship. Then the wife joined in and shared her
fears that her husband might leave her.

It's important to note that neither the husband nor the wife had verbally communicated their fears to the other, but both of them were aware of problems in their relationship. It's also important to realize that even if a person doesn't communicate openly about what is going on for them, particularly if it is of a negative nature, it will almost always be communicated one way or another. And holding back verbally can often be more destructive than being open and honest.

As we continued to talk, the woman admitted that she had been a slave to her fears, making them even more powerful than her love for her husband. When someone's fears run their relationship, it is not *just* because the other person has done things to create fear. Often, in fact, the person has brought a fear pattern into the relationship, and they may even have unconsciously chosen that particular partner because the familiar fear pattern would present itself. To some people, it doesn't matter if what is familiar is also negative, as long as it is familiar.

Many people feel more comfortable with their usual patterns of negativity because they have lived with them for so long. They stay with the familiar, rather than break through the limitations into a new and sensitive loving without restrictions. Freedom may frighten a person who has adapted to their chains.

To continue with this particular couple, I asked the woman if she often felt depressed. She said, "Yes, because it's a way of getting attention from my husband. When I get really depressed, he asks me what's the matter."

"Is he saving you?"

"Well, in a way, he's saving me from my depression."

I laughed, "In other words, you get depressed. Then your husband comes in on his white horse, saving you from your dragons of depression."

She smiled shyly, "Yes. . . ."

105

"And then he carries you off to bed?"

She giggled and nodded, "It's a great game."

The obvious game is that the wife gets depressed, and the husband saves her. The trap of that game is that the husband-savior will eventually tire of the game because the prize is just playing the game of more depressions and more savings, which will eventually deplete his savings account. The wife puts herself in the position of having to be saved from her own fears, which were fueled by his behavior, which stoked the embers of her conditioning, which . . . which . . . which, *ad infinitum*.

They were married about six months at the time we talked. I turned to the husband and asked why, with all of his doubts and insecurities, he had gotten married. He said he was approaching his mid-thirties and figured it was time to try it out. That seemed like a casual, almost flippant reason to marry, but he insisted that he loved his wife, did not want a divorce, and wanted their love to flourish.

The man also said that many of his previous relationships had been just sexual expressions. Then the woman started to indict males in general for approaching women solely as sexual objects and attacked her husband as a male chauvinist. Some of what she said may have been accurate, yet it is interesting to note—and I reminded her—that it is women who raised men. Why didn't our mothers raise their sons to honor and love women as full human beings and not as sex objects? Of course, we can keep going from one generation to the previous one, blaming that male or this female, all the way back to Adam and Eve, but we are still stuck with now.

In order to deal more effectively with what is going on in the present, how about taking an attitude that may solve difficulties rather than perpetuate blame? It can start with realizing that *all* of us have participated in dissipating the loving expression. Blaming one gender or the other won't change things. There can be improvement only when each of us takes full responsibility, regardless of gender or conditioned fears.

If a wife lives with constant concern that her husband is a "typical man," who will be attracted to other women sexually and will act on that attraction, then she also puts herself in the position of being run by her fear. Her next move may be to begin pulling her energy out of the relationship.

Then the man, who may have been looking at other women, but who always came home to the woman he loves, feels the energy loss, and perhaps he gets more than just a looking interest in other women. Then he may feel guilty or fearful that his wife may discover his temptations.

Please understand that the genders can very well be switched in this example. In fact, I know of a man so intent on being "honest" that he tells his wife that she isn't measuring up (to some fantasy in his head); then he wonders why his wife seems to pull out of the relationship. He has done much to create doubt, discouragement, and fear in her, and they both have become caught in a fear relationship, which may be heading for a crash.

Don't think that sharing so-called truths that are negatively inclined (e.g., "you're not enough," "you're too heavy," etc.) builds intimacy. Nor does blaming the other for fears experienced contribute to a positive, intimate relationship. True sharing, from the heart and with integrity, is not based on fear or on blaming someone else. It is a sharing in awareness. Yes, a person can say, "I feel insecure now, and it's my own creation, but just the same, honey, I wish we could hold each other right now." With this kind of honest sharing, supportive intimacy can very well be the result.

Just make sure that in the name of sharing, you are not dumping verbal or psychic garbage on the other person. Share your love, vulnerability, and sensitivity, and don't make the other person wrong. From that place, you can ask for any level of support in a relationship.

In any relationship, especially in an intimate one, focus on sharing a present-tense expression rather than on rehashing the past or attempting to establish blame for the other's past behavior. Someone once wrote, "The past is a bucket of ashes." By hindsight, everyone knows better. I suggest you use here-and-now sight. Use the information (from this book and from your living relationships) for the present because the past is history and the future will take care of itself.

When I once counseled a married couple, the man said he still lusted after other women and felt he was too young to settle down. I asked the man, "Do you want a successful relationship?" His reply was yes. He, his wife, and I continued to talk for a while, and then I asked, "What's the solution to the situation?"

The man responded with care: "The solution, as far as I'm concerned, is in sacrificing those desires, letting them go, and just giving my wife a chance to fulfill me instead of thinking it's better out there with someone else. Besides, even when I was single, I got tired of playing the field. Being married tells everyone I'm off limits, and, in a way, that's a relief."

We all laughed at his refreshing honesty and awareness, and I reminded him, "You can't be with all the women in the world. You don't have enough time or energy, even if they would have you, which they might not. What you can do is find all women through one woman. You can have erotic loving with all of the women through one—your wife. And I'm not talking about sex as something that has to do just with the physical body. I mean something even more meaningful—bonding with your wife in a deep, loving, caring way. Merge."

108

I explained to him that most women already know that they can't be fulfilled by having sex with a lot of different men. Women most often want one man who will commit to a relationship. Most women know that relationships work not just because of loving good sex, but that good sex is a result of loving.

You may read this, totally agree, and think you've got it, but that's not the way it works. For example, you can read a book about the different positions and steps in ballet, and you still won't be a ballet dancer. Obviously, the way to learn is to study and then to get up and participate, make mistakes, lose the rhythm, get the rhythm, time and time and time again, until one day you finally have it. That day comes as a result of thousands of hours of *practice*.

That is also the pattern for learning how to make a relationship work. Most people have had too many years of being conditioned by limiting beliefs to immediately activate a successful relationship. It takes practice—making mistakes, falling down and scraping the knees of your ego, and bruising the walls of preset limitations. Eventually, with enough commitment and caring, the walls of limitation may come crumbling down.

Many years ago, people said, "You can't take more than 50 percent of the blame in a relationship." People focused on blame and believed this statement (and perhaps some still believe it). As a result, they gave only 50 percent. I suggest that you look at your relationship, not from the point of view of blaming, but in terms of taking 100 percent responsibility for it. Don't worry about what the other person does or doesn't do. Just *you* go for it 100 percent. Some days will be better than others, and let that be okay. Just commit to it 100 percent, doing the best you can, and, in time, you and your partner will get the message.

The message is really simple: love each other.

Three Big Blocks to Communication

Judgment, fear, and guilt are three major obstacles to communication. It is extremely difficult to communicate information if one of those expressions gets in the way.

Part of communication is sending, or giving; part is getting, or receiving. If you tie a hook to your communication, you can be almost sure the communication will not be received. What's one big hook? Insisting on a certain reaction to the information you are communicating.

In that "room" within you where no one can get hurt, there is no room for hooks because hooks can hurt. In that safe-space environment, there is also no room for "shoulds," which might be dragged in by any hooks.

For example, if your lover is 20 minutes late to meet you and has kept you waiting, you might say, "You are 20 minutes late." Depending on your attitude, you could be doing more than just giving information. You could also be throwing out a hook that says, "You'd better be apologetic and endure my lousy mood because you caused it and you should suffer!"

There are other choices. I shared my attitude about this with an acquaintance who told me how annoyed he got when his wife was late one time. He said, "She knew we had a restaurant reservation and tickets for a play, and we both knew the curtain wasn't going to wait for her, even if she did have some great excuse for being late."

I suggested, "Let's start out with what you know. Is she a valuable human being?"

"Well, yes, of course she is. Do you think I would have married anyone who wasn't?"

"Good. Remind yourself of that. Do you think she knows you?"

"After eight years of marriage, I hope so."

"Do you think," I asked, "that she knows you have a low level of tolerance for being kept waiting?"

"She sure does. I've made that loud and clear."

"Is she very intelligent?"

"Very. What's this all about?" he asked impatiently.

"About you. Do you think your intelligent, valuable, worthwhile wife, knowing your temper when kept waiting, did that intentionally?"

"Well, when you put it like that, I guess not."

"Then here's a choice for a different approach. When she came running up to you, you could have said, 'What happened, honey? I hope it's nothing serious. Are you and the kids all right? I know you wouldn't keep me waiting unless it was serious.' In other words, you could have communicated your care for her and your children, instead of expressing your emotional impatience."

"Actually, you're right, because when we were eating and I had had half a drink and calmed down, I found out that one of the kids had been upset and she wouldn't leave it to the baby-sitter to calm her down. When I asked my wife what was wrong with our daughter, she told me that she missed Daddy. So my wife stayed a little later, assuring my daughter how much I loved her and telling her I would wake her when I came home with a hug and a kiss."

"How did that make you feel?" I asked.

"Like an ignorant, impatient clod. She was late because of assuring my daughter of my love. Now I just feel guilty for being impatient."

If you've ever felt like that, you can let go of the guilt. You can neutrally communicate the information to yourself so you can use the data to learn new behavior. The next time you start to have some emotional reaction, you don't have to give energy to being upset; instead, you can express your loving consideration for the other person. Know that only one thing counts: the loving that is expressed. Not dinner reservations. Not curtain time. Not anything but the love expressed. You can create your own "inner room" that is a safe space under any and all conditions.

People get into all kinds of traps because of communicating with expectations, saying something for an anticipated response. Perhaps you have said, "I love you" with the unconscious expectation of hearing, "I love you" back. If it didn't come, you may have felt that something was wrong. That's not communication; that's throwing out a hook. It happens in ways that are often humorous.

For example, not long ago, I lost weight and my body became well-balanced to the untrained eye. On a particular occasion, I dressed in a suit that was very well designed and fit my body well. I was feeling full of loving inside, and my exterior was appropriate to my loving state of being. I ran into an acquaintance, who said, "You look great."

"I know" was my response.

"Listen to *him,*" she said, as if what I had said was full of pride and ego. Her initial communication of "you look great" had a hook attached to it. The hook was an expected response of "thank you." When she didn't get that, she quickly communicated her disapproval and judgment of what I had said.

As for me, I laughed. I knew I looked great and felt even better. It wasn't a statement of pride, ego, or anything other than pleasant observation. She may have thrown the hook with her response, but I didn't have to accept it. I didn't have to deal with her judgment or expectations. I just laughed, loved her, and went on my way, looking great and feeling great.

I had created an environment within me for her to communicate anyway she chose, and I didn't contend with her reaction or interpretation. As a matter of fact, the next time I saw her I said, "How are you doing?"

She answered, "If I were you, I'd say, 'As good as I look.' "

"That must be terrific," I responded, "because you look that good."

She smiled. "Actually," she said softly, "I do feel great, and I'm ashamed to say it, but when I looked in the mirror, I said, 'Girl, you are definitely looking good.' "

We both laughed. "Why be ashamed to admit it?" I asked. "You look good because you do. You're not ashamed to say what a beautiful sunset that is, so why not admit your own beauty?"

"But that's not right. That's. . . ."

"That's nonsense," I interrupted. "Why put energy into a false standard? There is nothing wrong with perceiving your beauty."

She smiled coyly, "Do you really think I'm beautiful?"

I chuckled, "Do you?"

She glanced at her reflection in a nearby mirror. "Sometimes."

"Now?"

It was difficult for her, but she giggled and nodded. We both broke up laughing as we embraced.

The point of all this is that communication takes place with many people, including yourself, on many levels. Establish a relationship with yourself that permits the truth to be known—positive or negative, neat or sloppy, whatever. Once you establish that honesty–in–communication habit with yourself, it will be easier to be honest with others. Create that safe–space environment for yourself, and then you can extend it to everyone else.

If you do that, then the former blocks to communication—judgment, fear, and guilt—will become reference points. History. You can then communicate from that truthful place within you (without a hook), and you can also be more patient with others.

Communicating Past the Complaint

If you want agreement, try complaining about a situation or a person who isn't present. You're sure to get support because that's the nature of this negative planet. If you want disagreement, complain directly to the person whom you are judging as wrong.

"But isn't part of communication telling someone when they did something wrong?" a woman asked while I was counseling her.

"Give me an example," I suggested.

"Okay, sure. Just last Sunday, for instance, my husband and I were supposed to go out and spend the day together. That's sort of a tradition we've developed; we work hard all week, and Sundays are for each other. But last week, he wasn't ready to go until two o'clock in the afternoon. Half the day already gone!"

"What did he do the first half of the day?"

"Domestic stuff, you know."

"No, I don't know. What kind of domestic stuff?"

"He fixed a shelf in the closet and stopped a leaky faucet."

"Was that your closet and bathroom, too?" I asked.

"Of course, but he could have done it during the week."

"Did you ask him why he didn't?"

"Yes. He said he was busy working and didn't have the

time. But that's not the issue. After we finally left, we went to a museum for a little while and then walked around outside in the beautiful day. After only an hour, he said something about doing some work in service that would take about an hour and a half."

"Work in service?"

"Yes, you know, service. We each do things for others—the church, an orphan home, stuff like that—just for the fun of doing it."

"Sounds good," I commented.

"It is," she went on, "but the thing of it is, why can't he also be in service to me, to us? Why not make me a priority, particularly on Sunday, and especially because we agreed on it?"

"Did you communicate that?"

"Yes, and he said he could do his service after dinner. But Sundays, before and after dinner, have been *our* time. So we drove home so he could arrange to do his service. And, yes, I did clearly communicate how upset I felt about his choices."

"What did you do while he did his service?"

"Listened to music. Did the crossword puzzle. Caught up on some overdue correspondence. The truth is, I was relieved to finally answer a letter from my mother."

"So it sounds like you used the time constructively."

"Sure I did. But the thing of it is, after all that, I relaxed and went to prepare dinner, but then *he* was really upset. After I let go of it! He was hurt and angry with me for being so upset, and even though I was ready to cook and be loving, he was cold. So there's your communication!"

"No," I responded, "there's your lack of communication."

"What do you mean? I honestly communicated that I thought his priorities were lousy. I told him that Sunday is

115

our day and he had no right to ruin the one day of the week I look forward to as ours. I certainly communicated."

"What you did was blame, judge, criticize, and castigate. Worst of all, you denied him your loving. That's not the communication I'm talking about."

"I did all that?"

"There are better ways of communicating the same thing."

"Like how?"

"How about, 'Darling, I love you so much, and I cherish the Sunday time we have set aside to be together. I love you so much that I'll help with the shelf and faucet and maybe I can help with the service. And if you have to be away from me this particular Sunday, I love you enough to go out and buy some Chinese food and have it ready for you when you finish your service.' "

"But what about him?" she asked. "I was ready to let it go. I even communicated that. I said, 'Let it go, honey. I'm not angry or upset anymore.' *He* held on to the emotions, not me."

"Uh-huh. Isn't that a great Ping-Pong match you two have going? He did this, you said that, he reacted, and you 'self-righteoused.' The only thing you both communicated was separation."

"But I just wanted to be with him. I just love him."

"Then tell him that. Don't communicate through your emotional hurt, disappointment, or judgments. Speak through the mouth of just-loving him, look through the eyes of just-loving him, feel through the heart of just-loving him, and nothing can be denied to you. Even his holding on to the upset will dissipate in the warmth of loving patience."

Create that safe-space environment, particularly in the face of disappointments. Practice sharing the information—not from blame, but from loving. Not from fear, but from the courage of sensitivity. Not from guilt, but from admission and acceptance.

If you share from emotional needs, demands, and expectations, the communication can become negative and will usually be heard accordingly. Unless the person receiving it can transcend any negative energy you are sending, the response will most likely be negative. Is that what you want?

When you share the truth as perceived through your heart, you will communicate information that isn't negative or positive. It's just information. Then the person receiving it can deal with it as information through their heart. The response will most likely be heartfelt. Is that what you want? I imagine so.

The Ultimate Communication

The greatest social disturbances we have on this planet do not originate from people's being together and miscommunicating with each other; they originate from within each individual.

The person who can understand you the most, who can care for you the most, who can do the most for you—is *you.* The ultimate communication occurs within the relationship you have with yourself. To keep that relationship harmonious, you don't have to be perfect because that is not required on this planet–Earth level. What is required for a balanced inner relationship is to be in a continual state of self–education. Obviously, you are interested in that, because you are reading this book.

The next step is to activate what you have learned in order to tune in to the source of who you really are. An important part of activation is awareness. For example, there have probably been times when you acted out of your emotions in a negative way. It's those times that call for your awareness, and then you can activate what you have learned by stopping or even redirecting that emotional energy in order not to be run by it.

How do you do that? Well, one example is someone I know who is very stubborn. In the past, when someone disagreed with his position, he would dig in as if it were a do–or–die situation rather than listen, learn, and even give up his position. In time, he learned that all that got him was righteous anger, hardly a gift or benefit in his life. Eventually he figured out how to direct that same energy (which he used for stubbornness) by being more disciplined, and when those do–or–die emotions would rise, he would discipline himself not to react, but to just listen. Ultimately he learned how to use other people's input to improve his output, his work, his relationships, and his life. It all started with awareness. That's getting high enough to observe your behavior rather than being a victim of it. When you get the altitude to improve your attitude, that's high communication with yourself.

Some people experience pain or negativity and pray for things to get better. I am not denigrating prayer, but I do know that the answer to any of your prayers is already inside of you, in that place within that gives you the energy to get up every morning. It is called your Soul.

The energy of the Soul can often be felt as a sense of well–being, contentment, joy, and peace. It's not inactivity, but is directed action and aliveness. You are experiencing the energy of your Soul when you communicate to and from that place that is good–natured and free of irritation.

This inner balance can be maintained by committing to a state of inner communication, otherwise known as awareness. The mind is attracted to the physical world and will communicate through the emotions and the body, attempting to gain fulfillment through material things. The Soul, however, has a tendency to back away from worldly attachments. It also knows it is accountable for everything it does here. Your Soul, your true self, is responsible for what you create.

You are in this world to learn the highest form of communication, which is unconditional loving under all circumstances. Part of that process includes learning how to create wisely in order to bring about completion. In other words, don't start anything you can't finish in loving. Of course you, as a human being, will run into conflicts, confusions, disagreements, and divorce. Even those experiences can be concluded in loving. You can separate from someone physically and still know (and even say), "I love you, although our time together is not constructive for me." That's a far better communication than blaming the other person for a separation.

An important key to communication is that energy follows the thoughts you hold. Wherever you communicate and direct this spiritualized energy in the material world, things are manifested. That's both the good news and the bad news. If you have thoughts of success, not as a slogan but as a focus, then Spirit will actively support the attainment. That doesn't necessarily mean that you can sit in your house and pray to win a lottery ticket to be a millionaire and that Spirit will bring that forward. More likely, Spirit will—with your support—place you in the actions that can accomplish success. Sometimes it's a matter of thinking of success; then the thoughts of more education come forward, and then life will provide those opportunities.

If you have thoughts of negativity, that, too, can be made manifest. There is a saying that "what you fear

119

comes upon you." This means that if you communicate fearful thoughts, feelings, and attitudes to yourself, you are likely to attract that which you fear. You may even create the very thing you fear.

Is there a real source of fear? No. Is there real fear? Yes. It is inside you, and you are the creator of it. You give birth to your own fear. Under the fear, however, is life, which allows you to create and communicate whatever you want. This is the unconditional loving of Spirit, allowing you to communicate and do whatever you choose, with your body, emotions, and mind.

Your feelings about things determine much of what you do with your body, and how you feel is often influenced by what you think. If you're depressed, you may not feel like cleaning the house, mowing the lawn, or fixing the car, and you may decide not to do any of those things. Often, the feeling of depression is simply a lack of energy to move your body in constructive action.

Beneath that feeling is a deeper or, if you wish, higher communication that is more than your limiting thoughts or your feelings of depression. This is communication with the Soul, which is a part of God. The Soul radiates energy from the higher level of Spirit to your mind, emotions, and body; your mission is to learn how to get that communication. It is your attunement with this Soul energy that is the highest form of communication available to you. Once you experience that level of communication, you'll understand that no words can properly describe that "perfect" experience. Once you experience Soul consciousness, you'll want more. The good news is that more is always available.

There is a great commandment: "Love the Lord your God with all your heart, and with all your soul, and with all your mind, and with all your strength."[1] That means com-

1. Mark 12:30 (Revised Standard Version)

pletely. The other great commandment is to "love your neighbor as yourself."[2] This implies that you must love yourself first. When you truly communicate to and from loving, that high place which is always available to you, then the energy of God flows through you. Then you can reach out to your wife, husband, child, boss, colleague, teacher, student—everyone—and touch them with a simple, heartfelt communication, and they may transform right in front of you. Don't look for science fiction movie–like miracles. Just communicate loving, and you will receive loving. That may be God's primary miracle.

You were given life to have joy and experience it more abundantly, and if you're not experiencing that, look at what you might be doing to block yourself. Communicate that information to yourself with integrity, regardless of ego or preferences. Then use the information, not as ammunition for self–judgment, but as an opportunity to lift yourself.

You are a creator and, in that sense, an originator of communication. During your stay in this world, your highest calling is to communicate by every act of omission and commission a sense of loving. If you do that, then at the end of this short existence, you stand in that consciousness of loving where the ultimate communication just *is*.

2. Mark 12:31 (Revised Standard Version)

5

Your Relationship
with You

As I mentioned in the introduction, all relationships are ultimately your relationship with yourself and are often reflected by someone else. How well (or poorly) you get along with yourself will be directly mirrored by how you get along with others. Of course, if you are not doing well with yourself, you may not recognize this and may do the traditional thing—*blame it on someone else.*

I suggest you decide to break the patterns of unhappiness and helplessness by accepting a simple truth: when you leave that someone else (and it could be a lover, a spouse, a colleague, a boss, a parent, etc.), you are still stuck with whatever is inside of you that causes unhappiness. That doesn't make you bad or wrong. In fact, once you realize that the source of your unhappiness is within you, then you are in a position to change and transform that source.

Living on planet Earth can be an art based upon a scientific premise. The art is to approach life as a spontaneous experience. Part of the scientific premise is that you validate your experience.

The choices are to live in the present, be bound by the past, or be anxiety ridden about the future. That person you will meet tomorrow has nothing to do with what you didn't get from your father 14 years ago. Your mate's response last night has nothing to do with the restrictions imposed upon you 22 years ago. Your boss's attitude toward your project has nothing to do with the conditioned fear you brought in with the work. Yet you may go to one another, hurling conditioned ghosts in the face of emotional demands. Do you know who is relating? Not you. Not the original you. You may be relating through the ghosts of your past and, possibly, the fantasies projected into your future.

When you find yourself in emotional pain because he said something that hurt you or when you find yourself furious because of her behavior, guess who is out of balance. It is you, playing with your ghosts (or fantasies) in the haunted rooms of your life. When you were a child, you might have celebrated Halloween once a year and loved to be frightened. As a conditioned adult, you may be playing Halloween every day of your life, and if you are not in touch with love, it can be frightening.

Too many of us, too many times, make the pain of our lives someone else's fault.

> My husband didn't remember, my
> girlfriend ignored me, my mother
> shouldn't have, my father should have,
> my boss is making me crazy, the
> President did this, the Senate did that,
> it's all their fault and I'm so
> unhappy, it's *all* because of *them*.

If you do this, you are relating to *them* as cause and making yourself the effect. As in Pavlov's experiment, you gave them the bell to ring, and now you choose to be the dog that salivates.

I have heard so many people say, "But all I want is to be happy." Be happy. You can't buy a pound of "be happy." No psychiatrist, religious or political leader, parental figure, author of how-to books, or spiritual master can grant you the power to be either happy or sad. But you can be what you are now and get to what you want by doing what it takes to get there.

If that sounds confusing, let's talk about something specific, such as weight. Are you overweight, underweight, or perfectly balanced right now? One of the things you might want to *be* right now is honest. Odds are that you think you are somewhat out–of–weight, right? The obvious thing is that you can get to be thin, fat, or balanced, depending upon what and how much you choose to eat.

Relationships work the same way. It is yours to choose that which contributes to being emotionally thin, fat, or balanced. It is your choice to be happy or sad, in a fulfilled relationship or one of emotional pain. The table is set out there with sources that can make you thin with hunger for more or fat from gorging; or, by choosing wisely, you can arrive at a satisfying balance that is appropriately nourishing. (This includes your relationship with your body, yourself, and other people.)

Our "natural" state is loving. We don't have to wait for any divine miracle to occur. The fact that you are here, now, alive, breathing in and out, wanting to know how to become fulfilled, is a miracle in itself. The miracle is here, present, right now, if you are willing and courageous enough to avail yourself of it.

The miracle starts with acceptance. When we come to that place where we accept ourselves the way we are without judgment, we are then in a great position to give up any attachment to what we are not. It is those attachments to "what should be," to "I should have," and to "they ought to" that can produce anger, fear, resentment, rejection, or guilt—five major emotions that can block you from everything you want.

Give yourself whatever time it takes to come to that place of acceptance. We human beings have many conditioned barriers to transcend. Be patient with yourself as you seek to improve your life. Most important, be loving. There is never a good enough reason to take away loving.

Artist and Scientist

You can approach your life as an artist *and* as a scientist. Scientists take an action and then observe the results. If that action does not bring the desired results, they keep changing the action until they find one that does work. With this approach you can scientifically observe the results of your actions and move toward your desired result. Let's assume that the desired result—in this experiment we call life—is joy. If you are experiencing pain, you can change what you do. You can also observe which actions result in joy and expand on that expression.

As a creative artist, you can paint the picture of your life. If you see that some behavior or attitude does not fit into the artistic vision of your life, then it is probably not working for you. Have the courage and wit to change the artistic style, and creatively commit to another approach. Artists experiment and take risks in order to get in touch with the original expression inside them. Take the artistic risk and get in touch with you inside. How?

What ways have you tried? If your approach has been to blame "them," the results—the joy—may be limited. Look at everything you do, and ask yourself this question: "Does this increase my joy, loving, and abundance?" That is the only criterion to use, as you look at your life scientifically. These are the desired results of this experiment called life: increased joy, loving, and abundance.

What other methods have you used? Marriage and divorce and marriage? How has it worked when you have tried to change someone to fit your ideas and desires? Have they changed over the long run? Probably not.

How about going from affair to affair? Has that worked for you? Let me share a conversation I had with a person I counseled. This person said, "Affairs used to ease the loneliness."

"And now?" I asked.

"Now I want more."

"More what?"

"I don't know."

"All right, what do you want less of?"

"Less one-night stands."

"Why? I thought you said that used to ease the loneliness."

"Only for a moment, when I was embracing the other person."

"Who were you really embracing?"

"Someone who might love me forever."

"But did they?"

"No."

"Then you were embracing an illusion or fantasy."

"Yes. That's why I want to stop those one-night stands. The moments when my pain was eased weren't worth the emptiness that I was left with later. The aftertaste in my heart was terrible."

"Good."

"Good? You call that pain good?"

"Sure. Some pain can be valuable."

"How?"

"Sometimes you get so sick and tired of being tired and sick that you commit to changing. Then you can learn about what doesn't work for you."

"But I want to know what *does* work, not what doesn't. I want to know what to do to be happy."

"Well, let's look at relationships as though they are like a diet. When you avoid eating the foods that contribute to excess fat, getting slender is a result. The same idea can appear in relationships. As you eliminate those actions that cause disharmony in your life, harmony will result. Harmony is a natural state of being. You weren't born to live just in pain and negativity."

"Then how do I rediscover my natural harmony?"

"When you stop doing the unnatural things that block your harmony, your positive nature can reassert itself. It isn't so much that you'll find those things that work for you. They will find *you*."

"How long will it take?"

"Less than you think and longer than you want."

"I don't know if I can wait."

"Sure you can. You've waited this long."

"I'm running out of patience."

"In other words, you want to learn patience and you want to learn it right now."

This person laughed, realizing that there was no choice but to handle whatever came forward with a new approach calling for awareness and, yes, patience.

The difficulty in searching for happiness is that people often look for happiness in a source outside themselves. If they do find that someone else who they think will turn their life around, then they may start to live *for* that someone else. That path can lead to emotional enslavement and resentment. It's the approach that says on the one hand, "I'll do anything for you," and on the other hand says, "And you'd better love me for it." That's not loving. That's emotional blackmail.

If you do anything for anyone for any reason other than because, within you, you feel free and loving with them, then it may turn on you, making you feel negative

127

and at a great loss. Loss of what? Your power. You may give it away for approval, and there never is enough outer approval to make you feel worthwhile. You don't have to go outside to locate your worth. You do have to go inside to discover your worth.

It's called a place of integrity where the true self lives, that place where you do not deceive yourself, the home of truth. It could be a bloody place, a place of real severity, and it can often be involved with suffering. But the pain will dissolve, the wounds will heal, and peace will bloom, once you choose and commit to finding the source of your life's joy within you. Then the negativity is transmuted on the altar of your honesty, and the flower of your life blossoms in joy, loving, and abundance.

Those who would rather put off that inner investigation may continue to search for happiness out there someplace, focusing on acquisitions, food, or different forms of entertainment. They may change their jobs, their lover, or their hair more times than their hair can stand. They may move to another location, thinking they'll find it somewhere else—any distraction to avoid dealing with the true source of unhappiness, which is within. The paradox is that the true source of happiness is in the same location. But in order to get to the truth, a person may first need to travel through some deceptions and illusions. It does take courage, but the rewards are worth it.

When you feel dissatisfied, separated from yourself, or lonely, do you sometimes look for something or someone out there to make you feel whole, complete, or together? The fact is that no one and no thing out there can make you whole; all the distractions available don't ease the loneliness for more than a short time. If you ever feel lonely, you don't have to wallow in it or detest it. You can simply use the feeling as information, not as a reason to be devastated.

Loneliness is just part of your hidden hunger that wants to create. That need doesn't have to manifest as desperation; it can be an encouragement for you to expand your expression. It may manifest in such positive creative expressions as painting, cooking, swimming, dancing, gardening, acting, studying, writing, serving others, exercising, caring for a child with new, creative energy, and so many other ways.

These positive expressions are more than "weak substitutes" for what you may say you really want—Prince or Princess Charming, a particular job, money, or that possession. Rather than let those wants possess you, you can awaken now, and as you express your own creative beauty, you will attract that beauty and richness in others. Don't be a Sleeping Beauty, awakening only when you are kissed by the Prince. You don't have that long to sleep. Don't be a frog, awaiting transformation by the Princess's kiss. Be your own awakener to the beauty and power that are alive in you, right now.

You don't have to participate in the traditional dues of loneliness. We all know that loneliness can manifest in destructive ways, such as overeating; giving in to sugar, nicotine, alcohol, or drug addiction; driving a car recklessly; or indulging in meaningless sex. (My definition of meaningless sex is making love without loving.)

Loneliness, like depression, anxiety, and animosity, is a manifestation of your lack of oneness with yourself. Don't avoid the feelings of loneliness by seeking escapes outside yourself. Do use the information to go inside and connect to you as you are; then, from that place, choose expressions that take you where you want to go, as a person and as a lover, doing this as a loving gift to yourself and anyone you are with. Those expressions can be as simple as taking exercise or dance classes, reading to the blind, getting or giving a massage, playing, doing spiritual exercises, painting, giving yourself one day each week when you will say yes rather than no to all reasonable requests, and committing to seeing the humor in at least half of the events you consider serious.

Beliefs: Limiting or Freeing

Your relationship with yourself can cover a great deal of territory. If you define yourself as your physical body, that is one limiting definition. If you define yourself as your feelings, then you have another set of boundaries. If you define yourself as your thoughts, then you are, at least, extending your boundaries.

Right now, though, let's take a look at some definitions or beliefs that may limit the loving and joy in your life. You may let one or more of these beliefs run you, rather than give yourself freedom to have an enlightening relationship, first with yourself and then with others.

Here are some common limiting beliefs. See if any of these fit you:

- If I'm not achieving, I'm worthless.
- I must feel total loving toward everyone all the time.
- My childhood is controlling who and what I am now.
- I have to be married and have children to be a real woman.
- I should fit in, and I don't.
- I have to be what you want me to be in order to be happy.
- Success and money equal worthwhileness and being loved.

- I have to be perfect in everything.
- I have to be thin to be wanted.
- A spiritual person doesn't feel angry, upset, jealous, or greedy.
- I'm too old to start new things.
- It will be easier when I'm older.
- It will be easier when I'm married.
- It will be easier when I'm divorced.
- If there's upset, it's my fault.
- If there's upset, it's not my fault. (It's their fault.)
- I must always stay in control.
- I have to do it right the first time.
- I can't have a fulfilling relationship and a career at the same time.
- Making money is hard work and unpleasant.
- If they knew what I'm really like, they wouldn't like me at all.
- I have to make sure everyone's happy so I can be happy.
- If someone doesn't like or approve of me, I must be bad somehow.
- Someday my knight in shining armor will come and rescue me from all this.
- Someday I'll meet the woman of my dreams, and everything will fall into place perfectly.
- I can't be loving and spiritual and make it in the business world.
- I must be in love with someone all the time in order to be happy and fulfilled.

You may have found that at least one and possibly more of these limiting concepts are part of your belief system. Don't be discouraged if you find yourself involved with a number of these beliefs. If you start where you are, without judgment or guilt, then you are in an excellent position to live, learn, and love your way to the fullness of who you really are.

Are You Swinging on a Pendulum of Negativity?

At some point during our life span, we have felt a need to be loved, and for most of us, there was also a time when we felt an urge to express love, but we did not. For whatever reason, we just did not do it, and that is recorded in our being. When we do not express the love that is present, it shuts itself down. The next time that feeling comes up, it is much easier not to express it.

Over the course of time, many people effectively shut down their loving consciousness, the expression of who they are. And all of this happens in an absolutely justified manner. It usually goes something like this: "They don't deserve it. They'll just abuse it. They'll reject me. They'll hurt me."

It is possible that you have occasionally felt rejected, resented, and hurt. You may also have done all those things to yourself before anyone else could do them to you. It's very possible that during this self–rejection period, someone was experiencing a loving feeling for you. They were most likely waiting for some indication of interest from you—that smile, that warmth—which might have permitted them to make a move toward you. It could have been a friend, a potential romance, a parent, or a colleague. When there was no indication of interest from you, the other person may have been the one who experienced rejection. It's like a pendulum of negativity; after it swings long enough, you may forget who gave it the first push. You just continue to keep time in rhythm with a negative habit.

When you ride that pendulum, you have a unique ability to put out such rigid demands that no one can measure up to your standards (including yourself). How about letting people grow up around you (including your parents)? How about letting yourself grow up? Part of growing is to allow for mistakes. Part of maturing is to recognize the mistakes as experiences to learn from, rather than experiences to judge. That might be a living process of flexibility and adaptability, in which we not only permit but encourage one another's growth.

Humans do have an extraordinary ability to pick up and let go of things rapidly. Paradoxically, we also have the ability to form rigid patterns of behavior that bind us. When we are bound, we tend to judge others who don't see things our way. We may judge their gender, church, school, vocation, bank account, way of dancing, skin color, age, and cultural frame of reference. We judge them for not doing it our way. All of that judging springs primarily from our desire to justify our own feelings of separation, rejection, and hurt.

I suggest you live dangerously and ask that person, face-to-face and heart-to-heart, just one simple question: "Do you want to hurt me?"

The answer will most likely be, "Of course not." The intent is seldom, if ever, to cause you emotional pain, yet that is often the experience you choose to have govern your life. You may swing on that pendulum of pain that can eventually dump you into the chasm of depression.

If you do go into depression, you can handle it best by, first, making it permissible to experience a depression. That is, don't judge yourself for feeling depressed. As a matter of fact, you may as well enjoy your depression since you probably intend to have it anyhow. If you have an anxiety attack, you can assist yourself by getting in touch with that to see what it is really like.

Anxiety and depression are not caused just by thinking, so you can't solve them with just the mental process. When you are in touch with one of those experiences, you can follow it, not only to what may seem like the obvious cause—"He really pushed my buttons when he . . ."—but even further, to the actual physical location of that feeling: in the back, the stomach, the spine, the throat. There are ways to release the experience physically; you have that power and ability once you claim it. Once you own your feeling of depression or anxiety and get in touch with its source, you can transcend any life sentence of solitary confinement.

Get in Touch

Where do we come from and where are we going? If we stop and ask ourselves these relevant questions, we are less likely to be run by our ignorance. (Ignorance is just a lack of awareness.)

On your way to an appointment, if you get furious with a driver in a car going too slowly and you honk your horn in annoyance, you may be acting out of ignorance. Wouldn't it be interesting if that slow driver coincidentally assisted you in avoiding an accident about to happen two blocks down the road?

You may not know if the angry invectives you yell through the closed window (which can bounce right back at you) have to do with the driver, your anxiety over your appointment, or even some other situation in your life.

If you drive into a parking lot and are rude to the parking attendant because he doesn't speak your language fluently, is that because of him, or does it have anything to do with your having some traditionally conditioned judgment that says a good person always speaks your language correctly?

The obvious point is that so much of the time, people react emotionally to situations that aren't the real cause of the upset. By making the slow driver or the parking attendant the cause, you can be avoiding the real issue. If you would like to get in touch with a deeper level of what is going on with you, I suggest you take some time every day, early in the morning before you go out into that world, and run the pictures of your concerns through the lens of your awareness. During this process, you can see the choices, choose the action, and let go of anxieties. And in the evening, before going to sleep, review the day and run through events and relationships that may be pulling on your energy. What may come to mind might concern the last few hours, last night, next week, 20 years ago—it doesn't matter. Just give yourself time to get in touch with you. With no judgment and with compassion, take the time to review events, thoughts, and feelings; then take the time to read what's written in your heart.

You can call it contemplation, meditation, staring out a window—those are just names. The important fact is that when you give yourself time to be with yourself, you might be amazed at what comes up. You will most likely be relieved, too, because once you get in touch with what is truly contributing to the unease you feel, you may also get in touch with a way to complete and balance the action.

Clarify the unease before it becomes a dis-ease. Almost as a result of your commitment to get in touch, a solution can come forward. It is sometimes as simple as honestly acknowledging situations and feelings to yourself; sometimes it may be talking and being more honest with another. It could also mean writing a letter you have been promising yourself to write, paying a bill, making a phone call, cleaning a room, or studying for that test.

135

As an example of getting in touch with the source of emotional upset, a friend of mine has given me permission to share an event in his life that went like this:

> One morning I got angry with my wife because the eggs were too hard. From there we went into an argument about her doing the cooking and taking care of the kids and my working in the world, paying the bills, and doing the heavier physical work around the house. It was in the dead of winter, and our windows were frozen shut. My wife said that since I was in charge of the physical work, how about unfreezing the kitchen window so we could open it and let a little fresh air in. I was already dressed and on my way to work, with thick gloves on for the freezing weather. I went to the window, in the middle of our furious I-dare-you argument, to force it open. The window didn't give, no matter how much I pushed and shoved. Finally, in my impatience and fury, I "accidentally" smashed my gloved hand through the windowpane, breaking it, as I yelled, "There's your fresh air!"
>
> Twelve years after our divorce, that scene flashed in front of me. And the wild thing is that I saw what I was really angry about had nothing to do with the eggs. It was about the fact that our sexual relationship was not satisfying and neither one of us had the courage to talk about it. So we both lived a lie and made the eggs and the frozen window the subjects of abrasion.
>
> Then I looked at things a little further and recalled how my brother had had scarlet fever when I was a kid and I was shipped out of the house to my grandmother's, so I wouldn't catch it. During that time I was in the second grade, and I got all A's on my report card. I spoke with my mother on the phone to tell her about the A's, and she had to hang up quickly because my brother had a relapse. I experienced a great sense of loss then, but I told no

one about it, including myself. So we were all
seemingly ignorant on the surface.
   Thirty-five years later, I realized the loss I
experienced at seven had been perpetuated throughout
most of my life—by me. I had managed to subtly
interweave it throughout my life and my relationships.
   From my fear of losing a primary relationship again
(once at seven was enough!), as an adult I wouldn't
talk honestly about my sexual needs and
dissatisfaction. I wouldn't talk about my fear of
intimacy because I thought the relationship might be
taken away. I wouldn't get in touch with what was
really happening for me. Instead, I focused on eggs
and a frozen window.

This reminds me of a story I once read in *Aesop's Fables,* where the moral was "for want of a nail, a kingdom was lost." You don't need to wait, like my friend, for 35 years to get in touch with what is really happening to you each moment. Nor do you necessarily need to go back to when you were seven. Instead, you can recognize that when you are not expressing love, you may be living in a conditioned state that has little to do with what is happening or not happening in the moment.

Loving is a natural expression once you *move* past the conditioned cobwebs of the past or the imagined ones of the present or future. You don't have to understand or analyze a cobweb, and ignoring it rarely works. You can acknowledge and accept the fact that you—like all of us—have a conditioned filter, and then you can just *move, act,* and *do* that which allows you to *go through* it to the other side, where the natural habit of loving resides as the original you.

There are many things you can do to support your commitment. One is reading this book and putting into practice one or more of the suggestions. There are also support groups that can assist you in transcending your conditioning and transforming your approach to this thing called life. Some people participate in consciousness-raising organizations, from spiritual to educational in approach.

I know of some organizations that are designed to assist individuals in discovering and activating their original self. There are such forms, available right now, that can be of considerable value to you—as you value them. In other words, they can work for you as you work them. Seek them out, try them out, check out what works for you. How will you know if one process works for you? Be scientific. Ask yourself if the behavior that creates negative experiences has lessened and if you are creating more joy and abundance in your life. This isn't theoretical. I am talking about living a life that is truly filled with laughter and loving.

Relationship vs. Freedom

Many people have a hidden agenda about relationships. Some think an intimate relationship will curtail their freedom. They believe they won't be able to be themselves with someone close to them. So when they do get to be with someone, they perpetuate that belief by projecting what they think is perfect behavior. They are not being themselves. They don't share thoughts, words, events, feelings, and actions that they think might be viewed as less than wonderful. Instead of hurling a ghost of the past, they present an image of perfection that never did and does not now exist.

Putting energy into the perfection image (Mr. Wonderful meets Miss Perfect) is like replacing yourself with a factory-made robot built to fantasy specifications. Then it's a contest of which will break down sooner: the robot with the built-in obsolescence, or the all too human being with built-in obsolescence.

When the people are alone, what a relief! How relaxing! They feel so much freer when no one else is there because they are more themselves. In essence, they have given themselves permission to be the imperfect, marvelous, unique, ordinary human beings they are. At the same time as that can be wonderful, it can also further the belief that intimate relationships limit freedom.

That so-called freedom can sometimes get lonely, of course, and out of that loneliness, many people seek close companionship with another. Then, once again, each of them may present a perfection posture as they go together, live together, marry together—and divorce apart, when they discover that the other's perfection is just a pose.

No one can keep that perfection posture going all the time; it would be too exhausting. Eventually, we all have to let go somewhat and reveal the imperfect human being underneath the poses. Then (because of our perfection-conditioned expectations) when we see him or her as they really are, we may be off and running with disappointments, demands for change, criticism, judgment, and ultimatums. It's called separation or divorce. We may sit in our hurt feelings, justifying the separation with, "At least, now I can be free to be me. And I'll make sure no one ever threatens that again." Until the next time we get lonely.

If you have to defend your freedom, you are not free. If you are truly free, you have nothing to lose. Freedom isn't an object, nor does it have anything to do with pride or ego. Freedom as defined in *Webster's Collegiate Dictionary* is ". . . the absence of necessity, coercion, or constraint in choice or action; liberation from slavery or restraint or from the power of another." Only you can give yourself that freedom.

The same thing applies to trust. Rather than focusing on whether someone else is trustworthy, just make sure that you are. How do you do that? It starts with getting in touch with and listening to yourself. It involves appreciating your uniqueness and reaching past your image of how you might want to be perceived by others and yourself. It especially includes being honest first with yourself, even if it hurts (and in time it won't), and then with others, even if it hurts (and in time it won't).

Being honest with others isn't an excuse for abusing them verbally. It means being compassionate and sensitive to their culture and background, without imposing your ideas or necessarily embracing theirs.

Being honest means being aware and listening to your own truth. Beneath the ego and false images, each of us has our own truth barometer inside. If we connect to that, we are in touch with trust. Through that connection, we can know the truth of our own behavior and have insight into anyone else's. If we come from freedom and honesty when relating with someone else, the potential for love, joy, and growth is limitless. If we come from distrust and protection, the potential is likely to be negative.

For example, if you and I have a relationship, it means that something is going on between us—not just inside me and inside you, but also between us. In a free relationship, it's an energy flow in which we can gently "sit" in each other's consciousness. If we wish to speak, we can speak. If we don't want to speak, it doesn't mean we're angry or upset; it just means that we have the kind of relationship that permits each of us to do as we please, knowing that it will please the other person. That is freedom.

The clearest state of freedom in terms of relationships is that pure, open, honest communication, with yourself and another. In that relationship, intimacy is beautiful, accepting, humorous, and extraordinarily free because each of you embraces the freedom to be what you are. Each of you shares and loves the total human being. The beautiful traits *and* the imperfections are all part of the same package.

As you allow yourself the freedom to be who you are (it's called accepting and loving yourself with no guilt or judgments), you can also increase your ability to have a fulfilling, intimate, real, and lasting relationship with another person.

Freedom is loving and accepting with responsibility, loving yourself first and extending that love to others. Love never erodes; it is an organism that feeds off itself and grows. I suggest you water your loving plant with the freedom of honesty. Un-protect by sharing what is, regardless of considerations. You may be surprised to find that the person you care for has as many frailties as you. As long as you both share honestly, the human shortcomings are less likely to be held against the other; they become just part of the human process, like breathing in and breathing out. Even the life-giving breath sometimes doesn't smell as sweet as the life it gives.

There is really nothing to get out of relationships. Then what is the value of a relationship? *The value of a relationship is the relationship.* There is no other value. So don't look for what you can get from someone, but for how you can share your loving with them. When a relationship is based on your sharing your loving, you cannot lose. There is an unending supply of loving, and total loving is true freedom.

Beyond the Emotions

Love is difficult to define. Perhaps we can say that love is the essence that brings forces together and holds them in a position relative to one another. This applies not only to people. Even our cells might function together through that energy of love.

Many people think love and sex are the same thing. Ideally that may be so. In practice, however, we know that

141

love and lust are often confused, as are love and loneliness. When you ask someone, "How's your love life?" nine out of ten times, they will respond as if the question is about sex.

My love life has to do with my relationships to parents, children, colleagues, trees, mountains, a butterfly, a dog, myself, and God. The love I'm talking about is a state of being that encompasses all things, people, events, and experiences.

You can enjoy a mental love with someone just by listening to what they have to say. That has nothing to do with gender or sex, and it is an inner, active form of loving.

You can have a physical–emotional love that can involve sex or just the pleasure of being in someone's company. You can be writing and the other person can be reading a book, and physical–emotional love may be taking place in a beautiful, subtle manner.

In some relationships, spiritual love is present, the unconditional love that says, "I love you, no matter what." This type of love effects a harmonious balance that encompasses the mental, emotional, and physical expressions. In this love affair—where spiritual love is present—there is tremendous security. Neither one walks in fear of disappointing the other or being judged. There is only loving acceptance of each other's strengths and frailties. This is an alive, fun–filled, joyous relationship.

You may say, "That's exactly what I want, but I can't find a partner to do that with me." To find that outer partner, you may first need to find that partner within you. Do you love yourself, no matter what? Do you love yourself enough to enjoy not only your strengths but also your frailties? Do you love yourself enough not to judge or to impose guilt on yourself?

On a more specific level, do you shower because you want to be clean for yourself, or do you shower for the other person? Do you choose clothes to please someone else or yourself? Do you drive a particular model car because it will impress someone or because it pleases you? Do you laugh at someone's jokes because you find them funny or because you believe that's expected behavior? Do you make it all right to be part of the crowd at times and, at other times, to be different? (Different, not better or worse.)

Do you focus on your emotional need and look to others to give you love rather than get in touch with your own source of loving? Beyond your emotional need lies the love that already exists in you. Once you get in touch with your own inner loving, the external reflection can more easily appear.

Opportunity doesn't knock only once. Opportunity continually knocks as long as you are on this planet. The key that opens the door to joy and abundance is not emotional need. That emotional key may only open the doors of frustration, pain, and negative relationships. When you are in touch with your own source of loving, all doors can open. How can you be in touch when you are in the throes of sadness, depression, or anxiety? It isn't always easy, but it *is* possible.

This is not a how-to book in ten easy lessons. This is a *you-do* book in as many lessons as it takes to allow you to claim more of your loving heritage.

The first step toward loving is to accept what is going on within and without you. Just *wanting* to be happy, joyful, and loving doesn't quite do it. If you are feeling depressed, you have to be willing to be in the depression and go through it. On the other side, only one thing waits: the love that you deeply crave.

You may cry, "But I can't stand the pain and the loneliness." Yes, you can. There is a Spanish saying, *"Lo que no mata, enfuerza."* What doesn't kill you will make you stronger. You do not necessarily die from your depression.

143

How do I know? Have you ever felt depressed before? Sure you have. And here you are, reading this, alive. You didn't die, and you were able to get through it. You may have even grown stronger.

See if there are some areas where you can lighten up. One of the best ways to relieve depression or tension is with humor. It's never too late to have a happy childhood. Don't worry about your so-called enemies. I once saw a T-shirt that read, "Love your enemies. It will make them crazy."

Call on your humor in more situations and relationships. It is often humor that can release the burdens you sometimes carry. You can laugh at them enough so you won't be overwhelmed, maybe just "whelmed." Life does not have to be so serious. When I was a teenager, the air was clean and sex was dirty. Apparently that has now switched. You can see the dark side of that, if you wish, but I think it's funny. You see, we're all going to go through this life, one way or another. We are born and we die. What we do in between those portentous events is our choice. I'd rather laugh my way through life than cry. What about you? If you permit events and experiences to be *less* crucial, you may find easier ways than the traditional traumas on which to structure your life.

Some of us are Democrats or Republicans just because that's the belief system our parents passed on to us. Some are Catholics, Protestants, Mormons, Jews, atheists, agnostics, deists, or evangelists—just because they were brought up according to those belief systems. Some people are fat because they bought the belief that "you have to eat everything on your plate to be a good little boy or girl." (Some parents had a belief that a healthy child is one who eats a great deal.) Some people who are not married and don't have children feel guilty because of a belief system they accepted.

If you've inherited a belief system that is not working for you, you can give it up and move to what will work better. You may as well face the fact that the traditional way of "I love and need you and please tell me you love me and show it and prove it" just doesn't work all the time. There have never been enough ways to satisfy that bottomless pit of insecurity called "show me you love me." You may as well learn alternatives on the path toward a fulfilled, loving relationship.

You may be surprised to learn that negative conditions can actually lead to a positive place. On the other side of loneliness is a beautiful place called solitude. On the other side of rejection is the simply powerful place of acceptance.

You can compete or cooperate, stuff or flow, withdraw or nurture, withhold or share, ignore or care. On the other side of your emotional needs is the essence of love—not as a piece of candy that someone out there can give and take away, but as *you,* which no individual can take away. You become the gift and the giver. Sharing with another human being is not only possible but available according to your loving source. You need not be a whim of anyone else's love-quotient. As *you,* love comes out of you as a natural state, and that attracts the essence of others who may choose to share their love with you. Then it becomes a matter of each person sharing the loving that is inside of them. This is quite different from chasing after your affirmation by trying to take, pull, or demand love from someone else. When you give of the overflow, you are in charge of your life.

Love: Cause and Effect

People often feel a great deal of love toward someone, yet they may not know how to relate to that individual.

When someone dies, of course, most of us know ways of expressing love. We may send flowers and condolence cards, and we also offer love and support in many tangible ways. How about doing that when people are living? Why not send flowers to the living? Why not offer support and assistance during the living process? It isn't just a matter of words; it is a matter of choosing and then acting.

There aren't enough words to express love. Loving is a process of doing those things a lover does. Don't be just a TV or movie lover, imitating what you see on the screen. That is often make-believe, and real love is real. Be the real lover who does those things that really express you. You don't need to be concerned about the response; just express your own joy. If you are in loving, express that. If your partner is not in loving, your expression may invite them to share greater loving. Even hurt feelings can be cured by a liberal dose of loving.

Love is its own cause and effect. If we get our personalities out of the way, love will do exactly what's perfect in perfect timing. It's when we get in the way of love and expect certain responses or behavior that we can actually block love's action, rather than facilitate it. Left alone, love just bursts through.

Remind yourself that you don't have enough words, hugs, laughs, or tears to come close to expressing all the love within you. That love is very special and uniquely yours. Your need to share it is wonderful. But not with conditions. Love, in essence, is unconditional. There is no way of sharing that special energy other than letting it happen of itself. From chicken soup to a massage, from holding hands in a movie to taking a walk on the beach at sunset, from throwing snowballs to falling asleep holding each other—love does it out of its own process.

Are You Living by Your Experience or Theirs?

If you try to understand all of this with only your mind, you might get to nod your head or poke holes in this approach. Greater value can be gained through experiential understanding. That comes not just with intellectual understanding but with practice.

For example, you don't try to understand a pair of shoes you want to buy. First, you recognize a need or desire. You use data that are specific (shoe size, color and style to match existing outfits, cost, your financial position) and aesthetics (which change in time and culture); then you try them on, walk around in them, and look at that little mirror reflecting the possible purchase. If you have any past history, such as that shoes with three–inch heels create too much pain or that a certain shoe store is unreliable, you will let that influence your decision, if you are wise.

The same thing applies to relationships. Look at the data, your experience in the past: judgment, negativity, and trying to get the other person to change have probably not worked for you. Thus you must change the size and perhaps even alter the aesthetics. This formula suggests that the criterion is not out there, but is inside of you. The source of loving is not dependent on him or her out there on the shelf of the human market, but on your own shelf, the truth within you.

The next time you are with someone and find yourself leaning toward wanting him or her to fulfill you, get in touch with that. Are you once again recreating a relationship that is making him or her the necessary ingredient for living happily ever after? Are you getting involved in a

Cinderfella/Cinderella relationship where you are emotionally upset if they don't fulfill your needs? Are you blaming your dissatisfaction on a supposed lack in him or her? Have you fallen into that familiar trap, again, of playing Miss Perfect to Mr. Wonderful? That's newspaper today and wastepaper tomorrow, and it doesn't work today or tomorrow in that famous ever-after, either.

Instead of doing any of those tired and tiring routines, you can go within yourself and focus on those elements *in you* that are the essence of loving. Get in touch with the core of humanity *within you*. Get in touch with all the wonderful, real, positive elements of your own nature. Be in relationship to your caring, your empathy, your understanding heart. Do what it takes to evoke a loving awareness in you, and then see every human being (including the infamous "them") through your own love-colored glasses.

Practice being in relationship to your own experience—not your mother's, father's, child's, religious leader's, husband's, or wife's experience—just your own. Most people have a point of view about most things. Many of them dig into a righteous position and judge anyone who expresses differently. They may label those who disagree as wrong or immoral.

If you are not committed to relating to your own experience, you may buy into others' judgments and change yourself because of someone else's opinion of you. Doing that is buying into their experience and sacrificing your own. If one thing can block your growth and understanding, it is buying into somebody else's experience and opinion.

You may be with someone and hear all sorts of things that add up to what a terrible person you are, but that may not ring true for you. In such a situation, you have a number of choices. If you buy into their opinion, you are likely

148

to experience guilt, shame, resentment, anger, and all those other emotions that can lead to pain, disharmony, disease, and divorce.

You don't have to buy into anyone else's experience. You can listen, observe, and even find the person's presentation interesting, amusing, or entertaining. In addition, you always have the option of just getting up and leaving.

If the most important thing for you is to be the nice guy, the one everyone loves, the terrific person who has no enemies, then you may have a hard time doing any of that. The goal of wanting to get along and not have enemies, not even anyone who may disapprove of or dislike you, is impossible to realize. You cannot control other people's feelings, attitudes, and emotions relating to you. You can only exert control over yourself. Someone may choose to be your enemy or judge. How you react is your choice.

Your freedom lies in making your own choices. You do *not* have to accept someone else's vision of you. You do not even have to dislike them. If they dislike you, that is their negativity to deal with as they choose. You will be further ahead to leave their judgments for them to handle. You don't have to look to anyone else for approval. Go inside for the only approval that's true. Once you discover your own approval, with integrity and no illusions, you will then know what freedom is. And no one can take that away.

Walking Away From or Going Toward Love

Most of us want attention, particularly from a person we have designated as special. So we approach them in whatever terms are available to us.

Would you like a cup of coffee?
Something to eat? A movie? A dance?
A concert? A walk by the ocean?
Shoulders rubbed?

We all use attention-getting devices to investigate a relationship with that someone to whom we are attracted. Some call it flirting when we try to move from a lack of familiarity to familiarity with the potential of intimacy.

We sometimes do humorous things out of fear of rejection. We may make up signals that have little to do with reality: "If he smiles at me when I walk in front of him, I'll know he's interested in me." Then you walk in front of him, he doesn't smile, and you cross him off your list, thinking, "That snob. I never did like him anyway." Perhaps he had something in his tooth that made him uncomfortable smiling. By going with the signals in a script you wrote (but he didn't read), you may have missed just what you wanted. There may even have been times when you thought something like, "If she really wants to be with me, she'll answer the phone by the second ring because I told her I'd call tonight." On the third ring you hang up, while she may be racing from the shower.

People often spend as much time walking away from relationships as toward them, running superstitions and movie scenarios that only the author can read: "I'll be accepted if, by the time I get to the corner, that red car passes me, the light turns green, and the bus pulls out."

In approaching relationships, many people are afraid of being rejected. So they invent inferior signals that will warn them before they go too far. They would rather veer from the intended direction than suffer the pain of going all the way only to be rejected. In doing that, they read signals that are known only to them. As a result, they often avoid the rejection. They may also avoid the acceptance.

The Price of Approval

Once we receive the initial acceptance to investigate a relationship, then we may feel we have to get approval. The one you are interested in may say something like, "I'm interested in you, but you have to lose some weight." They are holding out the possibility of future approval (which is a present-tense way of saying, "I regret you now"). Their liking of you is obviously based on a condition of weight.

Your need for approval may be so great that you might go for the future-promise. The good news about that is if you are overweight, you may choose to lose the excess baggage and improve your health. The bad news about it is that you don't really know if you'll receive their approval when you do lose the weight. It is likely that they may bring up something else.

If you buy into those types of situations in relationships, you can be buying into a type of hell because you're damned if you do and damned if you don't. If the other person's affection for you is based on your behavior, you could save yourself a great deal of unnecessary pain by walking away. It is likely that once you meet the first set of conditions, the person is going to have others.

If you have the courage to support yourself, you might say, "I am really interested in you, and I am willing to look at things about myself that I can improve, but not on an either/or basis." If the person is ready to stick around and accept you as you are, then you have a relationship to investigate that has a chance. Remember this: if the ultimatum gauntlet is thrown down, you don't have to pick it up.

When Are You Worth the Affection?

Now suppose you go through all those steps of getting attention, acceptance, and approval from someone in whom you're interested. The next step is the expression of affection. Can you get it? Can you receive it? Can you give it?

You might figure that since you passed all those tests, you are *now* worthy of affection. On that testing level, you might be correct. On the reality level, no. You *were worthwhile* when you first started. You have always been worthy of love, but you may have looked for proof out there from someone else because you didn't believe—inside of yourself—that you were worthy to begin with.

You might say, "That's not entirely true. I mean, I started out believing I was worthwhile, but nobody else seemed to agree. So what good is it if nobody else says I'm worthwhile?"

There are over four-and-one-half billion people on this planet. Those whom you chose (and you did choose them, whether you know it or not) to reflect your supposed lack of worth represent just a tiny minority of fun house mirrors, which offer a distorted image of yourself. It isn't how you really look; it's just the mirrors you have chosen to reflect you. Out of four-and-one-half billion people, you chose them from that particular fun house, only it's not so much fun because you bought their lack of approval. Since no one of that miniscule minority out there loved you the way you wanted, you weren't worth loving, right? Wrong.

As long as you believe your approval and affirmation must come from others, you are unlikely to have it. It's hard to get approval if you keep giving it away to others. You can give away love with no expectations, and it will come back a thousandfold, but you can't give away your self-worth and expect it to come back. Granted, there are some people who do give it away with that expectation and demand. They give it to a male, a female, a religious figure, a political leader, a parent, their children, a book, or even scripture. It's called "I'll do what you demand, and you pay me with my self-worth."

You may dress a certain way that "out there" determines, behave a certain way that a book urges, drive a car that is approved, or behave in ways that friends regard as perfect, and you may even get the form of affection you crave—the *form,* but not the content. The *you* deep down inside knows that you probably got their affection for following the rules they made, not for being the original you. The affection is for fulfilling that traditionally conditioned concept of being a good boy or good girl. Therefore, the affection is always theirs to give *and* take away if you don't behave according to the rules of their game. It is never *yours* as long as *they* can give it.

The most devastating hurt that can be inflicted on you starts when you disregard yourself. Their power to hurt is only that which you grant.

Start with accepting yourself exactly as you are right now. Self-approval comes next, and if you don't approve, do what you have to in order to get there, and loving will take place. Love yourself with all your strengths and weaknesses; love yourself unconditionally. Anytime you run into expressions that no longer feel comfortable for you, you can change them, but remember to accept and love yourself through it all. Just as you are now, you are worthy of your own love.

From that place of worth within you, sharing can then be constructive, as long as you share *you.* From that self-loving place, you may say, "I want more joy, more love, more acceptance, more affection." You will get it from others when you give it to yourself, accepting yourself as you are right now. Accepting does not mean resisting change or ignoring desires or preferences. Just the opposite. But in order to change, the first step is to accept where you are right now, as information not judgment, as a place to start from, not as a place of guilt or resignation.

Do you want to quit smoking for them or because you run short of breath when you run up a flight of stairs? Do you want to lose weight for them or because you no longer feel comfortable with your body?

Do what you have to do in order to get where you want to be—slender, not smoking, whatever. Do it for and from you, and keep affirming and loving yourself on the way. With the weight that you intend to lose, with habits that you intend to change, keep looking into *your* eyes. You are worthwhile and lovable, whether you're slender or overweight, smoking or nonsmoking. Inside that human being, you will see the light of loving. That is no accident. That loving power rests within you. Sure, it may be somewhat covered because of some negative conditioning, but nevertheless, it is always there. The loving light exists in you right now, exactly as you are. Start from here and now, and you can do anything.

The power is in you. The decisions are always yours to make. Make them with *your* power *for you*. Acceptance, approval, and affection can more easily come from others when they come *from you to you*.

Intimacy: The Willingness to Share

After you have gained the attention, acceptance, and approval and have the affection, you may then be willing to share emotions and thoughts without editing them or running a hidden agenda. That's called intimacy.

In that context, there is acceptance of the mutual right to express anything. Getting agreement doesn't have to be part of the package; you just have the right to say whatever you choose to share.

In an intimate relationship, you and another have an agreement that you both have the right to be whatever you are and share whatever is present in the moment. This can allow each of you to go even deeper inside yourselves and express to the other person from that place. During that process, you may find yourself uncovering layers of defenses, which you built up over the years and which may have distanced you from other people. These may have been useful defenses at one time, and they may even have protected you under difficult circumstances. Now, however, with the one you love, that protection you use from your fear of being hurt may also "protect you" from intimate sharing. In fact, to continue rising in love, you need the ability to be open and share deeply.

The love and beauty of each of you will be evident in that sharing. It's called love; it's called Light; it's called Spirit; it's called truth. It is so strong that the essence can reach out and touch. A look can convey that incredible energy. From that place, strength is a natural outcome and risk is no longer frightening. All is permissible, and transcendence of fear, pain, and guilt is not only possible but likely.

Love That Works

There are many expressions that we call love, but there is only one type of love that is worthwhile and lasting: the love that enables us to become the lover to all people. Some people can take a lofty position and say, "I am a lover of the entire universe and everyone in it." They don't have to do anything much with that except bask in their lofty magnificence. (All that will do is give their ego a tan. I suggest they don't lie out in the sun too long, lest they get burned.)

Of course, you can narrow it down somewhat and say, "I love everyone in my country." Again, this can be a safe generalization that may require very little. You can get closer and say, "I love everyone in my city." How about bringing it even closer to home? How about loving the one to whom you are married? How about loving your boss? How about loving your child, your mother, your father, your brother, your sister, your boyfriend, your girlfriend?

If you cannot love a particular individual directly involved in your life, it may not be clear to lay claim to being a lover.

Some people go to great lengths to declare the level of their love: "I'd die for the love of you," or "I'd lay down my life for you." Instead of that, how about *living* for the love and expressing that in everyday events.

I recall the classic story of the man who wrote his lover a letter that went like this: "I love you so much I would swim the widest river for you. I would climb the highest mountain. I would fight a raging fire. . . . P.S. If it rains on Friday, I won't be over."

Unconditional love is like the postman's credo: neither rain nor sleet nor hail will delay his rounds. Nothing will delay unconditional love. If you qualify your loving expression, then you are probably not talking about unconditional loving. You are talking about a trade–off that says, "If you do this, I'll pay you with that." In other words, love for sale.

The love I am talking about is too expensive to sell. It's so expensive, in fact, that there is no price on it. There is not enough money or goods on the planet to pay for it. That's because it is truly free. It's the kind of love that says,

"I love you no matter what and will continue loving you."
That's the unconditional love I encourage because, frankly,
anything else simply falters.

Look at your life. Look at all the situations where love
lost because of the you–said–I–said arguments. Look where
love lost because of that's–mine–this–isn't–yours positions.
Look where love lost because of if–you–love–me–you–
would–and–if–you–love–me–you–should stands—and you
end up "shoulding" all over each other.

If you don't experience loving and try to give of yourself to someone else, you may very well experience lack,
emptiness, loneliness, alienation, or separation. When
those hurting elements appear, I suggest you look first at
your relationship with yourself before you blame the other
person. Ask yourself simple questions: Am I doing things
that are fulfilling me (that have nothing to do with the other
person)? Am I getting enough rest? Enough exercise? The
right food? Time with friends who are positive and supportive? Participation in cultural and spiritual expressions that
are nurturing?

When you live in a way that is uplifting to you on all
those levels, you are likely to attract people who have similar types of personalities, discipline, fun, and levels of commitment. Within such a commonly shared framework, a
loving comes forth that can work.

I am interested in a form of love that works. What
form of love works? When the expression and sharing evoke
an intimacy, a comfort, a security, and a safe place within
each other's heart, then it is working. When I know that no
matter what I do, you will just love me, then it is working.
When I know that no matter what you do, I will just love
you, that is love working.

Love will sometimes manifest in laughing at each other's frailties (not punishing each other with judgment or
insisting on change); sometimes, in leaving each other

alone for a while; sometimes, in making sexual love; sometimes, in falling asleep holding each other; and in as many more "sometimes" as there are human beings. There is no limit to the way loving can be expressed. That's a hint of the unconditional loving I am talking about, the kind that regenerates itself every moment it is expressed. Anything less than this kind of unconditional loving is too much less.

Unconditional love loves past your lover's behavior, not just up to it.

6

Spirit

In the thousands of seminars I have given throughout the world, the hundreds of audiotapes and videotapes made available to the public, and all of the books I have written, my sharings have primarily been from and about Spirit. The different chapters in this book are mostly for the reader's convenience because, ultimately, anything and everything is of God (and Spirit is the divine verb).

For decades now, people have asked me questions about specific spiritual concerns having to do with relationships. Some of the questions were posed while we were together at a retreat or seminar, and the process was recorded. Other questions were written to me, and my answer was mailed. This section of the book shall be presented in the form it occurred, that is, as questions and answers.

Regardless of what you read, if you can actualize the following, you will have learned all that you need to know:

> You are divine
> You are love
> Spirit is present
> You are the light
> for God is in you

(All the rest is commentary.)

Avoiding Negativity in Relationships

Question: How can I be sure I'm not creating negativity or imbalance for myself in relationships?

Answer: There are a few criteria. One is, don't go into guilt. Do you know why guilt hurts people? It is the most intimate, personal, emotional response you can have that you can't really share with anyone else. You can tell people about your guilty feelings, but that's telling, not sharing.

Guilt is your own homemade product. If you feel guilty, you have ingeniously set up a tribunal of judges within you. Depending on your cultural or religious background, you could use the Bible, Koran, Kabala, Bhagavad Gita, or maybe even a saying on a building: "To Thine Own Self Be True." Whatever it is, you have used an outer source as your reference point for how you should behave. If you don't behave according to that, you judge yourself and then create and eat of the guilt.

That's not to say that any outer source is wrong for you. It's not the source itself; it's what you do with it. Anything or anyone may offer wisdom—in words, signs, symbols, and experience. To bow down to writing on a wall or in a book can be ineffective, to say the least. To worship the writings in your own heart and manifest the heart's action in your life is to live in the true power. If you are going to do something, instead of feeling guilty, you may as well enjoy it. If you are not going to enjoy it, don't do it.

Another way to avoid creating negativity in relationships is to follow a simple guideline: don't hurt yourself and don't hurt others. The most effective guideline might be to do everything as an expression of unconditional loving. If you do that, you will not create imbalances that you will eventually need to resolve.

When I say unconditional loving, I am talking about the essence of kindness, care, and consideration—for yourself and others. If you act out of word-level justification (which I urge you to avoid) rather than heart-level caring, then negative energy can become part of your life's baggage. If you are going to do something that may be less than loving, I suggest you take responsibility for it instead of invoking righteous reasons for your actions because, no matter what you say, what you do is always your creation.

There is that part of you that knows honesty, that knows integrity. Regardless of any words, if you act without being in relationship to the knower inside of you or without owning what you do, you may be acting dishonestly.

Dishonesty forfeits divine aid. I am not talking about honesty as defined by culture, environment, or legislation. In these cases, a lot of things that are illegal or "just not done" today may be legal or allowable next year (legislatively or culturally). Not too long ago, for example, the vast majority of people in the United States considered it sinful for a man and woman to live together without being married. Such cultural definitions of sin are often seasonal.

There may be a time in the future when women outnumber men ten to one. Perhaps under those conditions, polygamy will be legalized, changing a cultural point of view to support a condition of a new reality. Those issues, however, have little to do with the honesty I am referring to. I am talking about being in relationship to your essence, the original you that, in and of itself, is integrity and honesty. Doing anything less is avoiding the relationship.

Example of Unconditional Loving

Question: You talk about unconditional love a great deal. I understand it intellectually, but I don't really know if it's possible on this negative planet. Can you give me an example of unconditional love—and I don't mean the spiritual end, but when things are rough on this nitty-gritty level?

Answer: A long time ago, I worked as a psychiatric technician in a hospital. There was a particular patient who was about 90. He was all skin and bones, with large sores on his backside; his eyes were almost closed because of an infection, and there was an unpleasant odor in his room. Most of the nurses and orderlies didn't want to have anything to do with this man because he was expected to die soon. So I asked the doctor and nurse if it would be all right for me to take care of him, and they gave me permission.

I rolled him over and then cleaned his sores with hydrogen peroxide and held warming lights near him for lengthy periods; within three weeks, the bedsores were gone. I powdered him, diapered him, and cleaned out his eyes.

At one point, he started talking to me. I was surprised because this old man hadn't talked all the time I had been working in the hospital, and I had assumed he had lost the power of speech. He explained that he didn't want to talk because the rest of the staff treated him as if he were already dead. We had a beautiful conversation that went like this:

He said, "You were a little rough a few times when you rolled me over."

I replied, "Be thankful that I rolled you over."

He laughed and said, "I am, and you still rolled me over a little hard."

I smiled and asked, "Why didn't you speak to me sooner?"

"Because I thought if I said something, you'd stop."

"That's because you don't know me," I said.

"I do now," he said, "and that's why I am telling you to take it easier." We both laughed.

I made sure his room was one of the best smelling ones in the hospital. I made sure his bed was fresh. I knew he wasn't going to live much longer, but while he was living, I made sure he had the attention he deserved as a human being.

When he died, there were no sores on his body. When he died, he was content that somebody had cared enough to take care of him. He died while I was in the room with him. He said, "I would like to die now."

I said, "Well, not until I give you a hug."

He smiled, "What do you think I am waiting for?"

I hugged him and he died, and I cried. Then I washed him because I cared enough.

You see, unconditional loving doesn't care about smells, looks, or any other condition. It's just a matter of "love 'em anyway." That man is dead, and he's also alive in me and, perhaps, in you with whom I share the experience.

Marriage As Conditional

Question: I've been married and divorced a few times, and although I am aware of and appreciate unconditional love, I have not been successful in finding a marriage partner to express unconditional loving. Is it possible?

Answer: It may be foolish to marry somebody for unconditional loving. You probably married for conditional loving. People marry for everything from sex to sharing, from fun to finances, and everything in between. Those are *conditions*. I'm not making that wrong. I just suggest that each partner know and agree to the conditions. Then you

can enter into the conditional loving and love it unconditionally. If you make the spiritual choice, you live above the
conditions. By that I mean, as your body walks through
this world, you walk with God.

You may not like hearing this, but all that you do in
this world doesn't seem to amount to much. Here, it matters little what you do; what does matter is your expression
of unconditional loving, within a conditioned relationship,
within a conditioned world.

Do the best you can with what you have to work
with, and do what it takes to get God's guidance and
grace. Then, even conditional relationships can work unconditionally.

Relationships and Spiritual Law

Question: What about relationships that are involved
in spiritual law?

Answer: Spiritual law says that you and the other
(employer, partner, lover, teacher, etc.) have come together
to bring about something that will be of great benefit to
everyone. You have to function upon faith in that relationship because there will be very little knowledge in your
head, intellect, or mind, although there may be a deeper
knowing. Spiritual law is written in the spiritual heart. Two
people—when abiding by that spiritual law—fulfill the divine law, which is based upon total trust and faith in each
other and in God. Spiritual law is the most beautiful, dy-
namic, fulfilling law that exists.

The opposite of that is human law. Human law without spiritual law can result in relationships in which you
confine, misuse, and abuse the other person. That's a hell
on earth.

You can also *choose* to be involved in a spiritual relationship wherein you submit to the spiritual law, which is often just a matter of getting out of the way. The energy is so pure and powerful that the action will be done its way. You may think that sounds as if you do not have free will, and from that viewpoint, you are right, because this relationship under spiritual law was created long before your ego–need of free will. You, in essence (and I do mean essence), have chosen to be God's instruments and examples in fulfilling the spiritual law.

Emotional Loving and Spiritual Loving

Question: Is there a difference between emotional loving and spiritual loving?

Answer: Emotional loving often involves emotional blackmail: "Do it my way or else I will withdraw my love. Agree with me and I'll shower you with my love." Spiritual loving is unconditional: "I do love you and will love you no matter what." In this form of loving, there is fulfillment because there is no hidden agenda—just 100 percent positive expression. It is complete in itself because it is not dependent on the actions of the other person. You love the person beyond their behavior.

In emotional loving, there are often lack and unfulfilled desires that range from lust to depression. Spiritual fulfillment is not to be found in someone else no matter how beautiful their body or mind is. These things are not designed to bring spiritual fulfillment. The Soul and Spirit are the vehicles for that.

The "Perfect" Relationship

Question: Is there a perfect relationship available, or is that just a romantic fantasy?

Answer: If you mean by "perfect" that another person will fulfill all your wishes, dreams, desires, and requirements, the answer is no. In any relationship, you give away something and you get something. The thing for you to determine is whether what you get makes the giving worth it. For instance, you may give away your sense of privacy and your being able to do anything you wish without having to consider another person's response. What do you get in return? Perhaps companionship, sharing, a partner who is fun to be with, or . . . any number of things.

Then, of course, there is giving that which always makes it worth it: namely, loving.

Relationships with other human beings are imperfect, and we come to each other to share and learn on the way to perfection. Where is perfection? It is not in relationship to each other, but in relationship to that which is perfect. That already exists, and your job is to find the way. How? Practice, and you'll find the perfection of Spirit within you.

Love, Marriage, and Spirit

Question: How do love, marriage, and Spirit integrate? Or do they?

Answer: When unconditional loving is involved, they certainly do, although not necessarily on the word level. As an example, let me share a story about my father and mother.

Years ago, my mother used to say to my dad, "Do you love me?"

He said, "I give you my paycheck."

She said, "I know, but do you love me?"

"You're the woman who raised my children."

"But do you love me?"

He said, "I've always put food on the table and clothing on the kids' backs, and you've never been denied anything."

"But do you love me?"

"Why do you want to know?" he asked.

That was their game. Later on, I asked my mother if she thought Dad really loved her. She said, "Oh, of course he loves me."

I said, "Then why won't he tell you?"

"Well," she said, "because then there'll be nothing for us to debate over."

After laughing, I said, "When he does finally tell you that he loves you, what are you going to do?"

She said, "I'll die. I'll just up and die."

I said, "And he'll just die, too."

"Well, probably."

Many years later, I was talking to my father and asked, "Dad, is Mother the woman for you?"

He said, "I don't know, son, but a long time ago, before I was born, I was in a counseling session in heaven or wherever. I knew that there would come a crisis in my life that would involve an incurable illness. And only after I had gone through an operation for it would I know if she was the one for me."

I said, "Isn't that kind of hard to handle?"

He said, "No."

"How come? I mean, what if you discover that Mom is the wrong one?"

"That may very well be, but I won't abuse her. And if she is the right one, I wouldn't want my right one abused either."

Years later, my father had a cancer operation, and afterward he wasn't given much longer to live. My mother said to him, "Oh, honey, you know I'm really going to miss you. I don't think I can stand to live here without you."

My father said to her, "I just want you to know one thing."

She said, "What's that?"

He said, "Well, I love you."

She said, "I always knew that."

My mother died within six months, before my father. After her death I said to Dad, "You remember a long time ago, when you told me about the right woman?"

"Yeah. Your mother's the one."

"Well, you know, you told her you loved her."

He said, "Yeah."

I said, "She told me once that if you ever told her, she'd up and die."

He said, "Well, your mother's really a strange woman. She's always taken care of the family. So she's gone over early just to get the 'house' set up for when we get there."

I said, "Any particular thing you have in mind?"

He said, "No, she always knows what that is. She's always known exactly what's right for all of us to do in terms of the family."

"What are you going to do now that she's gone?"

"I'm going to visit with you kids, and we're going to do a lot of things we haven't done before. I'll also spend a lot of time missing your mother." (He had told her many times over the years that he loved her.)

Responsibility and Freedom

Question: When two people are involved sexually, physically, emotionally, mentally, and financially, but one is

168

participating in a spiritual life more than the other, what is the spiritual relationship or the connection between these two people? What is each person's responsibility?

Answer: The person who is more aware has (within) the inherent responsibility to teach the one who is not as aware. By "more aware," I mean more aware of the greater potential. The responsibility is inherent in the relationship. It's similar to your seeing a little child start to run across the street into the path of a car; you'll yell at the child to stop. It is a teaching consciousness that makes you say, "Watch out for the car!" To teach doesn't mean you must sit and do the ABCs with the child. You just respond within the inherent relationship on a need-to basis.

Be cautious, though, because many people want to be in the position of the teacher, particularly in a one-to-one relationship. The truly aware one *demonstrates* the level, not by assuming the position of authoritative instructor but by *living* the qualities of understanding, acceptance, and cooperation.

That doesn't mean that the other person is necessarily going to learn, but the one who is more aware is inherently obligated, spiritually, to teach them. Teaching is not thrusting the information down someone's throat to make sure they get it; it is presenting the information, making it available. It's like offering a smorgasbord. You lay out all the food (various choices) and say, "Eat what you want, when you want. I have prepared the table and put out all the things I know."

If the person says, "I don't want any of it," the more aware one knows that is fine. It was just inherent in their position to make the presentation. If the teacher does not accept this and goes into recriminations (e.g., "You should have tried harder; you should have done better"), producing an atmosphere conducive to guilt and all the discomfort that goes with that, then it is the teacher who needs the lesson. Rather than produce guilt and its results, it may well be for both persons' advancement to break off the relationship.

If, like two ships that pass in the night, you are not going to make the connection, you might be further ahead to own up to it immediately. It can be as simple as saying, "Look, I just don't think we're seeing eye to eye philosophically, culturally, educationally, or generally. Something is not working, and if neither of us can move from this position, it's better that we separate."

At that earlier moment, perhaps neither one has invested very much of their energy, so going in different directions may be the cleanest thing that can be done. It's when we invest our energy that we are more likely to get upset and resort to such emotional responses as "you abused me and misused me." We are actually saying, "Your energy did this to my energy." I suggest you become ecological about the use of your energy.

The person who is relatively lower on the awareness scale has an appropriate position as that of a taker. They must take a great deal into them before they can give back. For example, a youngster of two isn't expected to give a great deal to the house because children are busy taking during their early years. Even if they awaken in the middle of the night, you will take them a glass of water or walk them to the bathroom. At that age, it is natural for them to be involved in taking.

There are cases, however, when a parent might say, "The kid at 35 is still taking." Actually, it is the parent who has contributed to keeping the 35-year-old a "kid" because what was necessary was not taught. It is the parents' responsibility to gradually wean their child away from that taking consciousness in order that the person learn to stand up in their own strength. Otherwise, they will always lean on the parental figure.

Perhaps one person comes to another and says, "You are more spiritually advanced than I. Would you teach me?" An appropriate response might be, "I can teach. Can you learn?"

Most people can hear, but not everyone listens, and not everyone learns. An indication of learning is a change in behavior. This change may manifest physically, emotionally, mentally, or spiritually. If learning takes place, a change in behavior results.

Learning is not to be confused with awareness because awareness isn't necessarily a factor of learning. Awareness is more a factor of letting go of conditioned reactions and permitting the experience to take place without resistance. This may or may not be observable.

Responsibility of Infants

Question: Do infants have any spiritual responsibility when they are born, or is it all for the parents to handle?

Answer: The answer is yes to both. Infants have a responsibility to fulfill the destiny of their birth. The first breath that infants take establishes their involvement in the planet, nation, region, state, city, and, certainly, the family. That is a spiritual given that all children assume when they are physically born.

Of course, infants function within the reality of their physical and mental development. Since they cannot yet communicate with words, they will yell and cry to get things they need. They also have the ability to create a need in the parents and other empathic adults to pick them up and love them.

Spiritually and physically, the parents have to assume enormous responsibility for that God-force that is known as their child. For some parents, that is a difficult realization.

"God-force? You mean that kid, who always dirties the diapers and screams, is a God-force? That's hard to believe!"

I suggest that parents look at all the "diapers" they themselves have dirtied when they have screamed and yelled in anger and negativity. And, reasonable or not, each of the parents was also born onto this planet as part of the God-force.

The Spiritual Path

Question: If the mind has limited awareness, how can I know if I have left my spiritual path?

Answer: If you stray from the expression of loving (inside and out), you are leaving your path, and the result can be experiences of confusion and anarchy. Again, I am talking about unconditional loving, which includes acceptance, not the kind of emotional loving for which people have killed. That isn't loving; that's killing.

The only things needed from you in your life are involvement, commitment, support, and expression of loving. That's all, and on this planet of negativity, that's a lot.

Difficult? For most people most of the time, yes. Does it have to be that way? Not at all. Once you choose to have a relationship with the loving inside you, it gets easier and easier, until it is so easy that loving becomes a process of breathing in and breathing out.

At this point, loving becomes the source of life, which is the greatest truth you can recognize, because the plain fact is that *loving* truly is the source of life. The most valuable relationship you can have to life is to accept what is, regardless of your preference. It's also the smartest approach because what is, is—regardless of your preferences, emotions, or judgments. So you may as well accept that relationship.

Loving in the Face of Negativity

Question: How can I remain spiritual, or loving, when someone I love directs accusations and emotional upset toward me?

Answer: If you don't like what someone says, just go to another level of consciousness until that person is finished. For example, if that person is coming from a highly emotional place, you can go higher within you and just listen, observe, and not defend your position. If you wish to give information in response, do it from a neutral place of presenting just the facts as you see them. From that higher place, called altitude, you are then in a spiritual position without getting caught in emotional, defensive postures. It isn't easy at first, but then again, things of value aren't always easy. You might start by silently calling for the spiritual Light to fill, surround, and protect you (even while someone may be accusing you). And then send the Light to the other person. It may not work perfectly at first, but with enough practice, love, and Light, even a "rock" can open.

Working with the Ego

Question: Is the ego spiritual?

Answer: The ego is part of the mental and emotional process and can be either your friend or your enemy. Actually, it may be a friendly enemy because, ultimately, the ego (as well as the mind) is the "enemy" of the Soul. If we utilize the ego correctly, however, we can have it function *for* us, being aware that as soon as we give our power over to it, it can destroy us. It will destroy us by making us believe we *are* the ego. It will turn us away from our greater awareness of who we truly are—the Soul.

I have heard people say that the thing to do is kill the ego. That isn't possible. The wisest thing to do, when the ego tempts you into negative reactive patterns, is to bypass it. Then you can make the ego your servant, instead of letting it be your master.

Some people choose to bypass the ego by prayer (asking or talking to God), meditation (waiting for the answer), contemplation, or, my preference, spiritual exercises, which is a process of actively participating in God's energy. By extending yourself and sharing yourself with God in the spiritual form inside, you create the opportunity to connect from your Soul to the great Oversoul, the supreme God. In that place, the ego does not exist.

The unconditional loving that exists in the Soul realm can be expressed on this level, too. It's a matter of loving someone past their behavior. That "someone" also includes yourself.

Question: If the ego is a tool to use in the physical world, how do you keep it working with you in a positive manner rather than a negative one?

Answer: Through devotion, commitment, and consecration, which will result in liberation.

Divinity vs. Misery

Question: How can I call myself divine when half the time I'm actually miserable?

Answer: If you call yourself anything less than divine, you are not dealing in truth. Feeling miserable is just an emotional reaction to a divine lesson being offered to you. From the same experience, a person can either get depressed or become inspired.

You don't think so? How about rain? Something as specific as rain can cause people to run the emotional gamut from loving joy to terror and can create abundance or disaster.

A romantic couple walking in the rain can make the experience special. People in a drought-ridden area in Africa can make rain a welcome, almost religious experience. A family living on the Mississippi River in the wet season can regard rain and the resultant floods as a tragedy. At the proper time, a farmer may regard rain as a needed blessing; at other times, when the crop is about ready to be picked, the farmer may see a heavy downfall as disastrous.

As another example, when Columbus discovered that the world is round, do you think everyone went for it? Some people considered Columbus a heretic and wanted to hang him. For others, it was the end of their entire belief system, and they were ready to kill themselves. Other people embraced the information, feeling liberated.

Similarly, extreme and different reactions occurred when Einstein explained the theory of relativity. To some, that was an incredible release into even greater freedom. To others, however, it was the destruction of belief systems and a threat to self-worth.

If your self-worth is based on a belief system, you will almost certainly be liable to depressions and misery. If you are willing to let go of any conditioned attachments to a belief structure, however, you can then let in a freedom of choice, a freedom of living that lets in the positive. Then loving, abundance, and joy are always available to you. You just have to let go of enough limitations to let in what already exists. That is the divine. Anything less is a matter of attitude.

You can call yourself a lot of names, from depressed to

miserable, and those are just labels to support your attitude. Does your attitude encourage restriction, limitation, and negativity? Or does your attitude create freedom of choice, living, and abundance?

Father, Son, and Holy Ghost

Question: What is our relationship to the "Father, Son, and Holy Ghost," and how can that be expressed by a human being?

Answer: The Father is the creator. The Son is the manifestation of the creator and also a creator, and the Holy Ghost is the sustainer of the manifestation of the creator and of the Son. Those definitions are in line with some religious and spiritual beliefs. Other credos may have a different concept of the creator and the form through which such energies are commutated down to human beings.

Regardless of form or labels, the way we get God's energy is through loving, in the kind of loving in which there is no negativity. For instance, if a child passes gas, are you embarrassed and judgmental, or do you accept the act as a natural function? No judgments.

When you feed an infant and food gets all over her face, her hair, her clothing, and you, do you get impatient? Not likely. You probably love the child, coo, and play games while you aim for her mouth and laugh, seeing the humor in the sloppiness and nourishment. No judgments.

If you really want to experience God expressed through a human being, spend time with a child when both of you are relaxed. Eating, talking, walking, playing—just be with a child, and you may recognize God.

Perhaps one reason children appear closer to God than

adults is because they are not yet as conditioned with judgment and guilt. They are closer to the state of innocence and acceptance. You, as an adult, can participate in that. Perhaps you can find the child within you. Not making anything right or wrong and not feeling guilty can be an attitude that promises the highest relationship you may have. That relationship is you with Spirit.

Be Jesus or Me?

Question: I have heard some religious leaders tell me to "act and be like Jesus." As much as I love Jesus, I also understand that I am no saint, yet I feel that if I don't "act and be like Jesus," I'm fated to go to hell. Can you help me?

Answer: We are each totally responsible for our actions, in the spiritual sense. Jesus already did Jesus. You are not here to live the life of Jesus Christ. You are here to live *your* life, to balance *your* life so that your expressions and attitudes are of a positive nature, and to express *your* unconditional loving in ease as well as under duress. God is in you, as in Jesus. All you have to do is become more aware of God in you.

Jesus was 100 percent aware of God, 100 percent of the time. But don't use that example of total awareness as a cause for comparison, guilt, or self-judgment. Instead, use it as a frame of reference for what is possible, a reminder that you can constantly work on your awareness as you go through and enjoy life. And no matter what goes on with you, remember that life is to be enjoyed and that you can bring forward the will, wit, and loving to do it.

When You Know What's Right for Others

Question: Sometimes I really know what is right spiritually—not from an ego or mental level, but from experience and loving. The problem I encounter is when I see friends ignoring what they know and not acting out of their awareness of the right thing to do; I often judge them and want to shake them into shaping up. Should I push them into more appropriate behavior or just ignore them?

Answer: Part of the reason I seldom tell anyone that they're doing something wrong is because what they're doing may not be wrong *for them*. It may be necessary for them to do whatever they are doing in order to get the learning that the experience is offering, so they won't have to do it again.

I suggest shifting more into the role of an observer and just leading by example rather than from an attitude of "you should do this." If a person asks you, of course, you can give advice. Even then, however, I encourage you to always give at least two choices while you offer information from a neutral, loving place, without trying to force or manipulate them to do a certain thing.

Then allow the person the privilege of taking the information and changing it to fit their own circumstances and personality. After they've done that, you can stand back and let them be free to work it out in their own way and to gain the value of their own experience. As an analogy, you can try telling a young child how to walk, but the child still has to experience falling, getting up, hanging on, falling again, and scraping the knees. The child learns to walk through experience.

It may help you to hold an accepting attitude if you

understand that a person's behavior and struggle are preparing them for the next level of their existence. That struggle is a strengthener. I let people have it.

Taking Your Space

Question: What does the expression "take your own space" mean to you?

Answer: I heard that expression many years ago and observed people seeking physical space or space to express themselves emotionally. I also saw others use that expression as justification for negative behavior toward someone else.

To me, the only space that anyone can really take is that which is inside them. That space is not so much taken as it is discovered. The process of discovery that is most effective, from my experience, is spiritual exercises.

Changing Names

Question: If I change my name, will that help my professional and personal relationships?

Answer: If you change your attitude, it will do a lot more. But if changing your name helps you change your attitude, get with it. You may be overdue.

What Is the Light?

Question: I have heard many religious and spiritual leaders refer to the Light. Is the Light from God or from a person? And if it is from God, what relationship does a human being have with it? What are we supposed to do with the Light?

Answer: The Light is a form of energy emanating from God. Just because people talk about the Light doesn't mean they are empowered by it. The Light is not something to be received or offered on a word level. If you are connected to the Light, you don't have to do anything. Just be.

The Light may "disturb the comfortable and comfort the disturbed."

Abortion

Question: Is abortion spiritual or not spiritual?

Answer: There are times when a person has set in motion a spiritual action that may not match their conscious decisions. If a woman becomes pregnant and consciously does not want the child, it may be that she contracted *spiritually* to have that child. Of course, the woman (and the man, if possible) must work out things like that according to their own consciousness.

Are There Miracles?

Question: In our relationship to God, are there such things as miracles?

Answer: There are miracles, but people often are unaware of or misuse these divine gifts. This reminds me of the story about a man lost in the woods. He had been living on berries and roots for three days, and his life-force was wearing thin. He fell on his knees and prayed, "Lord, if you rescue me, I will devote my life in service to Thee." Within a short time, two hunters found him. The man said, "Forget it, Lord. These hunters found me."

Every person experiences miracles every day but often doesn't recognize them. This lack of recognition may eventually lead a person to believe that all gifts are a result of their own personal power (ego), while ascribing all painful experiences to God. When people are asked to explain a devastating hurricane or flood, they often say, "God's will." How come no one asks anyone to explain a beautiful day, a rainbow, or a hummingbird?

Thinking vs. Doing

Question: I've read a lot of spiritual literature, and no matter how much I read, think about it, or even understand and agree, my life still doesn't improve. Is there something I'm missing?

Answer: Yes, your life. Reading, thinking, understanding, and agreeing can be just intellectual gymnastics unless you get up and do something about the information. Activate it. How? By *doing*. In order to live your life, you must get up and handle things. Don't just think about something because just thinking doesn't handle things. Doing gets it done. And when it is done (anything from taking a test to doing the dishes to fixing the car to doing spiritual exercises), the act of doing may have contributed to freeing you. You can become free because the energy inside you is no longer directed toward feelings of despair, grief, or guilt because of incompletions and undone things. Once you have tasted the freedom of the movement of Spirit, you most likely will not turn back. Doing produces freedom.

Living As an Example

Question: I try and live my life as an example for others, but, frankly, I'm not sure of the value of that because most people are selfish and unappreciative. Do you have any clarification that can help me?

Answer: Live your life as an example to yourself. Don't bother trying to live as an example to anyone else. That's opting for either an ego stroke, which has no lasting value, or crucifixion, which might last longer than you wish. Claim your own life and live it from that inner understanding that is yours, regardless of the opinions or behavior of others. You can still be considerate of others, you can still abide by the laws of society, and you can still live and demonstrate a life that has the integrity and loving unique to your inner awareness of Spirit.

I suggest that you don't do good to try to impress your spiritual teacher, your boss, your wife, your husband, your child, or anyone else. If you are going to do good—and I pray you do—then do it for the sake of doing good. Do it because it's the correct thing to do. Don't pick up litter only when someone is watching. Do it if you're the only person in sight because it's the thing to do. The one who expresses good without any other motive is the one who receives of the blessings.

By doing good for its own sake, you will find a satisfaction in your heart that is beyond words. It may not satisfy your mind or emotions because they sometimes do not understand the levels of the heart. The saying "virtue is its own reward" is accurate. Live a life that has virtue, integrity, and love in it. You will find that is enough.

The Value of Suffering

Question: I once heard you say that if we knew the value of suffering, we'd never ask to have it removed. What does that mean?

Answer: Whenever we're at our very best, we often think we don't need God. And at those times, we rarely find God. When we are suffering or at our very worst, however, that's the moment we call out most profoundly to the Lord for help. That is often when we've discovered the Lord. In those times, suffering has been a purifier because it has actually brought us to the place inside us where God exists. It can also awaken us to a wisdom that brings a resolution not to do those things that brought the suffering.

So suffering, from my way of looking, is often the angel that stands at the gate of hell. When I see that angel, I recognize the potential for suffering if I continue doing things the way I have been. So, faster than I can tell you, I change what I'm doing. My experience with suffering is such a powerful reference point that I no longer create more suffering for myself.

When you look at it from that point of view, suffering is a marvelous reference point. If your pattern is that you have to get so sick and tired of being tired and sick, well, then, that's one way to go through life. But if you're smart enough to look ahead and realize that you don't have to do that which you know will cause you suffering, that, to me, would be preferable.

Does God Really Provide?

Question: Is it true that God will provide everything I need?

Answer: Yes. Everything you *need,* not necessarily want. What you need are experiences that will awaken you to the state of unconditional loving that exists within you right now, at this moment. Too many times, people relate to God as some sort of great "bellhop in the sky," and their prayers are a conglomerate of "gimmes." The gifts of creating opportunities are already yours. As someone once wrote, "What you are is God's gift to you. What you make of yourself is your gift to God."

Desires

Question: Is there a relationship between Spirit and our emotional and physical desires?

Answer: In a way, yes. When you are searching for love, emotionally or even sexually, you are actually attempting to find and connect with your Soul. Out of loneliness, you may focus your search on this physical level, longing for someone. But the yearning is really for your own Soul. Until you recognize that, you may seek happiness through any number of substitute gratifications, which are only temporary. In other words, they are illusionary and cannot bring the fulfillment you seek. Only Spirit can do that.

Celibacy

Question: I know that certain East Indian religions advocate and practice celibacy and that some Westerners, such as priests and nuns, take vows of celibacy. Does that mean that sex is contrary to spiritual progress? I am married, with children, and I love my family. But I also love God, and I don't want to do anything that will block or dissipate my connection with God.

Answer: The only thing contrary to spiritual progress is to act without loving. Those groups and individuals that practice celibacy find that this expression works for them in terms of conserving and directing their energy. That is not to say that married couples are any less spiritual because they express their love in sexual intercourse. There are many paths to God, although there is but one God.

If loving and acceptance exist in your actions, then God is part of all you do, including breathing, elimination processes, eating, sexual intercourse, prayer, spiritual exercises, and service.

Sexuality and Spirituality

Question: Is it true that the energy creating the urge for sex is in the same area of the body that gives impetus to spiritual expressions?

Answer: No, the area called the "third eye" (which is located in the middle of the forehead) is the spiritual center in our body. But sexuality and the *creative* urge of Spirit reside close together, in the band in and around the body from just above the navel to mid-thigh. Because of their close proximity, many people confuse the creative surging of Spirit with sexual urges. If they release the energy through sex, they may not experience spiritual fulfillment.

Some people have said that the sexual urge is the most powerful drive on the face of the planet. This isn't so. The imagination is more powerful. Consider how long the sexual expression lasts. Then compare that to the amount of time spent anticipating sex or thinking about it afterward. The imagination, the creative force, is the primary drive, and sexual expression is a result, not a cause.

It is often difficult to differentiate between the drive

toward sexual creativity and the drive toward spiritual creativity. People often misinterpret the urge toward Spirit— and perhaps we should be grateful for that, or some of us might not be here.

As I have suggested many times, if you are going to have sex, do yourself a favor and have it with the most enlightened person you can find. That doesn't guarantee anything, of course, but each of you may have a better chance of sharing honesty and affection.

Question: If the husband and wife are both involved and active spiritually, will this affect their sexual life?

Answer: The love bond can take place without sexual intercourse. Intimate sharing can be a touch of the hand, a loving massage, or falling asleep holding each other or even with the toes touching. When this bonding takes place (assuming that both partners are active in doing spiritual exercises and service), then it is possible for the interest in sexual intercourse to lessen.

A side effect of this situation can be that one partner, having received of spiritual inflow, wants to share the sexual expression as a comforting device. If the other is less interested in sexual intercourse, the first might feel unloved because they're not sharing sex as they did before.

In actuality, their love may have become elevated from carnal desire to spiritual fulfillment. This is not rare; it often happens to people who are spiritually involved. It takes mature adjustment to accept that when a couple first live together, they may have sex every night for six weeks. Then the expression may gradually decline. After two years, for those actively involved in spiritual expressions, the couple may have sex as seldom as once every three months. Eventually, it could decrease to, perhaps, once every two or three years. To some, that may sound drastic, but when the spiritual energies flow, the energies exchanged during the sexual act are not needed in the same way as during the early months of marriage.

If the man and woman can make this adjustment, recognizing that the frequency of the sexual act is replaced by the frequency of Spirit, it can be a relaxed, enriched time in their life, as they share energies of the highest nature.

Question: Are spiritual men generally less expressive sexually than nonspiritual men?

Answer: Spiritual people can be "bedroom athletes" because, for some, the level of physical lust is still running them. They often function biologically on misinformation, thinking their lust will be satisfied by sex. This lust cannot be satisfied until and unless the hunger is turned toward Spirit. Then it is no longer lust, but a give–and–take. As you give to Spirit, you shall receive a thousandfold.

If people marry for sex, the marriage may last, perhaps, six months. If they marry because of an emotional attachment, the marriage could continue for a couple of years. If the marriage is based on intellectual sharing, it could last a lifetime. And if the marriage is based on Spirit, it can last beyond this life. Then the use of terms like "Soul mates," "twin Souls," "Soul rays," and so on, may apply—not literally, but as an indication of an eternal oneness that is primarily spiritual in nature.

Question: Is there a contradiction between the sexual expression and the spiritual expression?

Answer: When a couple express unconditional loving through sexual intercourse, the two can rise to the greatest spiritual oneness attainable in the physical body. Sex becomes an exchange of energy, a way to fulfillment and completion.

If, however, the premise of the sexual act is other than unconditional loving, a person may feel let down, depressed, and empty after intercourse.

Sex in itself is neither good nor bad. It is just another way to balance and fulfill yourself in your physical expression.

Does a Woman Need a Man?

Question: Does a woman need a man in order to be spiritually fulfilled?

Answer: Nobody needs anybody else to fulfill himself or herself spiritually. You may find that it assists you to be in a group that is committed to a spiritual process and that can support you when the powers of negativity come calling. (Being on this negative planet, you can be assured that such doubts and temptations will come.) I encourage those in spiritual communion to share—everything from counseling, to eating together, to a walk on the beach. In the company of your brothers and sisters in Spirit, you can receive spiritual support, refreshment, and, most of all, loving acceptance. In that process, you can constantly reconnect to the Spirit that is you, and when you are connected, there is no need for anything else.

The fantasy called "I must have a Soul mate in order to be complete" is really a travesty. Theoretically, it is possible that your Soul might be fragmented into as many as 256 different parts throughout the planet, and each part is whole and complete, as is a hologram and as a cell of the body has all the replicates of the rest of the body. So it is possible that you could be living in many different existences, and when you all die, you meet and merge into a higher frequency, combining all of your experiences and existences.

Rather than spending your energies looking for your "Soul mate," I suggest you do what it takes to go into the oneness of Spirit. It's called practice, being with others of a similar commitment, and participating in mind, body, and Soul in your spiritual growth.

How Women Deal with Negative Energy

Question: You have said that the man releases negative energy into the woman during sexual intercourse. Does the woman hold on to the man's negative energy—released during sex—or does she transmute it?

Answer: She releases it during her menstrual period. (He also releases positive energy.)

Question: How does a woman deal with this energy if she has gone through menopause?

Answer: Through wisdom in the choice of a partner and with a mutual upliftment of each other toward God.

Male and Female: Spiritual Difference

Question: Is there a spiritual difference between men and women?

Answer: There is a difference in the way men and women process spiritual information and spiritual experiences.

In the lower realms of life (below the Soul realm), we function by the law of reciprocity. For example, if you push something "this far," it has to come back "this far." It's give and take, a balancing of positive and negative energies.

189

On the whole, when a woman receives spiritual information, her basic nature is one of receptivity. She receives. The man's basic nature is thrust. He gives. (Of course, there are exceptions to this. We know many women who also give and a lot of men who also receive.)

In very broad terms, when a man receives spiritual information, he primarily wants to move into the world and make a kingdom financially. When a woman receives spiritual information, she primarily wants to educate her family. So if you educate a man, you educate an individual. If you educate a woman, you've educated the entire family. Consequently, you will often find more women than men in most spiritual movements.

Once the Spirit moves in a man and woman, within a relationship, the woman can very well be the man's "quiet." No matter what travails he may have endured, she has the ability to allow him to enter into her quiet, calm, and peace.

Ending a Relationship

Question: What if I am in a relationship and want to end it but the other person doesn't? Does walking out mean that I am free, or will I be carrying any unresolved energy of the relationship with me?

Answer: Your first responsibility is to your relationship with yourself. As soon as you took your first breath in this world, it became your responsibility to keep breathing. If I were in a situation that I clearly determined was completed, I would share the information with the other person. I wouldn't do it as an emotional diatribe: "I'm complete with you. You make me crazy, so I'm leaving whether you like it or not!" I wouldn't use words if the subtext didn't involve loving acceptance. If you say, "I understand your point of view," but underneath you are thinking that he or she is stupid, then your subtext is judgmental and of little positive value.

I would simply share something to effect of, "I no longer wish to be involved with you sexually, physically, emotionally, mentally, or financially. If there's anything I can do to support you during this transition in ways that work for me, I would really like to help." If the emotions arose, I would be very careful with myself and the other person. I would not be emotionally blackmailed, nor would I do this to anyone else.

Spiritually, we are all involved whether we like it or not. We choose the level of our physical involvement with others. Some people choose to stay with the other person for a period of time, assisting them, teaching them, helping to make the transition to separate lives more positive. Even under those circumstances, it is always valuable to be honest to the point of saying, "I'll be with you for a while, but three or four months from now, I'm going."

At the end of that time, I suggest you keep your word. If you stay because you don't want to hurt your partner—yet you know that it is over inside you—that's like cutting off a dog's tail a little bit at a time. If the experience is really over for you, then be true to what's in your heart, keep your word, and leave the relationship. In this way you can depart with a loving acceptance and a feeling of completeness.

Maintain integrity within yourself and with your partner. Relationships of honesty and integrity may not always evoke happiness at the moment, but they surely plant seeds of joy, which can blossom in the very near future. And that plant is perennial. Once you align with the integrity within, joy does bloom eternal—not as a slogan, but as an ongoing, alive, and nourishing process.

Path to Heaven or Hell?

Question: A friend of mine comes from a religion different from mine and insists that he'll go to heaven. But he says I'll go to hell if I follow my path.

Answer: In reality, there is no path. There only *is*. There is no distance to travel because you are already there—rather, here. It is only a matter of awakening more to the divine heritage that already is.

Regarding your friend's concern, all people have the right to their own adventure with the truth. You can declare that right, for your friend and for yourself. The fact that different people have different religious beliefs and different bibles isn't the issue. The only issue that is worth anything is a person's own living scripture.

I suggest that you keep focused on your own spiritual experiences. Someone may say that you are wrong and urge you to participate in their experience. If you assume your life is wrong because you are not expressing yourself their way, then you are in a relationship with *their* experience, not your own.

Regarding heaven and hell, those concepts differ according to various religious or spiritual beliefs. Heaven will take care of itself if you (or anyone else) worship God in prayer, meditation, spiritual exercises, or contemplation—whatever form connects you to the unconditional loving of God.

We can have different rituals and different names and definitions for spiritual ideas. If they are accompanied by unconditional loving, they can all lead to God. Some people call it heaven. Some people call it the Soul realm. Words and labels are not the experience by itself. They are invented by human beings to help people approach that which cannot be understood by the mind with the mind. It

SPIRIT

isn't the mind that transcends death. During that passage, there is but one God, who has no name and who resides in a place that has no label because it is all-space, all-loving, all-ways, always.

I encourage you to live in relationship to your own experience and not anyone else's, regardless of their charisma or energy. At the moment of passage from this physical realm (known as death), are you going with a name of God on your lips, based on someone else's experience? Or will you move to higher realms with the essence of God in your heart, based on your own experience?

The Reason for Life

Question: Is there a specific spiritual reason for our life?

Answer: You are here to find out who you are, to move to the Soul realm, and eventually to become a co-creator with God.

Are We Our Brother's Keeper?

Question: Do we really have a responsibility to be our "brother's keeper," or is that just wishful thinking?

Answer: Each conscious person has a responsibility to other human beings. Even if you don't know them, you have a responsibility to them. That doesn't mean that you have to do whatever someone else is doing. If someone is digging a sewer, you don't have to jump in the ditch and dig with them, although that, too, is an option you can choose.

Your responsibility is to support people, offer encouragement, and hold a positive, nonjudgmental attitude toward others. And whatever you do (or don't do), make sure it is your heartfelt response.

In your taking responsibility, don't impose or be a dogooder when it is not asked for or welcomed. If you have any doubts, ask. If you can assist others physically or financially and if it is comfortable for you and the other person, then, by all means, do it. Sometimes, however, you can just be with that person, in peace, quiet, and loving, and that energy can accomplish a great deal in itself.

Tithing

Question: I've heard of the concept of tithing. How does tithing work? Is it the same as making a donation?

Answer: Tithing is quite different from giving a donation. A donation is above and beyond tithing. Tithing is a spiritual law; the payment is a spiritual payment.

One of the fundamental human errors is materiality, manifested mostly in terms of concern for the monetary value of things. Greed, by its very nature, strikes against the Spirit inside. Once you come from greed, there is never enough in this world, and there is always a hunger for more.

You can break the greed pattern by tithing, giving 10 percent of your personal wealth to a spiritual organization of your choice. You can also give from corporate wealth if you own the company; thus the company tithes. Tithing is an action that is specific as well as mystical and invisible. When you tithe, Spirit recognizes that you handle abundance well and grants room for even greater abundance; that is mystical.

Sharing your abundance joyfully is a form of glory in the human being. That glory attracts more things. So when one person becomes free of materiality, it can become like a positive infection. Instead of greed infecting honest people, honest people affect the greedy.

"As You Sow, You Reap."

Question: Does the expression "as you sow, so shall you reap" apply just to spiritual things or to this physical level, too?

Answer: Most people think this expression means that if I do something to you, it will come back to me. That action does not come under the "as you sow" law, but under "an eye for an eye and a tooth for a tooth," the exacting of payment.

In understanding "as you sow" from the biblical point of view, we can go to Galatians, where there are references that explain this concept:

> Brothers, if someone is caught in a sin, you who are spiritual should restore him gently. . . . Carry each other's burdens, and in this way you will fulfill the law of Christ. If anyone thinks he is something when he is nothing, he deceives himself. Each one should test his own actions. Then he can take pride in himself, without comparing himself to somebody else, for each one should carry his own load. *Anyone who receives instruction in the word must share all good things with his instructor.* Do not be deceived: God cannot be mocked. A man *reaps what he sows.* The one who sows to please his sinful nature, from that nature will reap destruction; *the one who sows to please the Spirit, from the Spirit will reap eternal life.* Let us not become weary in doing good, for at the proper time we will reap a harvest if we do not give up.

Therefore, as we have opportunity, let us do good to all
people, especially those who belong to the family of
believers.[1]

In other words, "as a man soweth, thus shall he reap"
deals with the spiritual instruction and God. That law is of
Spirit and enacted in the spiritual realms. "An eye for an
eye" is of the Old Testament. With the dispensation of
Christ, however, it is the spiritual law ("God cannot be
mocked; a man reaps what he sows") that is the first estate
of man and woman.

You may sow things in the physical world, and they
may disappear. That which you sow into Spirit and God
won't be mocked. You can't sow into Spirit on a word level.
You *do* the spiritual things (i.e., prayer, meditation, contemplation, spiritual exercises, service for the joy of serving, etc.), and these will strengthen you.

Sometimes when people enter into intimate relationships, they start fighting and attacking the other person.
That is participating in the law of cause and effect on an
unaware level because most people, when they fight, are
really asking the other person for more Light and love. We
often fight because we want the other person to show the
God-form to us—not the terror of God, but the loving of
God.

It would be intelligent to avoid expressing from feelings of lack. Silence might be a better choice. In the silence,
perhaps you can come to a true understanding of your need
for love. You don't have to express that need in anger, frustration, or impatience. You can express your need without
accusing another of failing you, without judging someone
else. If you learn to do that, you can avoid the as-you-sow-
so-shall-you-reap syndrome, the law of cause and effect.

1. Galatians 6:1–10 (New International Version, emphasis added)

What you do in silence, God will reward. No one may see it, but you shall be rewarded with the strength and fullness of what you have done. How will you know that has taken place? Go inside. Take the time to be in your own quiet place. Listen, watch, sense—and you may travel the spiritual worlds in awareness.

The law of cause and effect is experienced (consciously or in unawareness) by all human beings. When you connect to the spiritual center within, it will most likely give you more opportunities to create peace rather than disharmony. As you awaken to the peace center within you, you can share that energy and contribute to peace in this world.

You must have Spirit in this world if you are going to have peace in this world. Individual peace is the prelude to world peace. Individual peace starts with you, regardless of what anybody else does. You can have peace in relationships by not entering into conflicts. We can have peace in this world by not entering into war. "As you sow, so shall you reap" is too often interpreted as a negative warning. It can also be a highly spiritual action wherein a positive action leads to a positive result.

Hold the image of what you want. On the physical, imaginative, and spiritual levels, create and express that which is positive and uplifting, and then you can reap what you have sowed: the abundance and joy that is your heritage.

Is the Soul Unique?

Question: I like to feel that I am unique, even in God's eyes. Is my Soul unique?

Answer: The unique statement is that we are what we are right now because everything we've done prior to this moment equals "right now."

There is a uniqueness about the Soul; everyone has one and everyone is part of that energy. There is, however, something "more unique" about the Spirit that fills the Soul. That Spirit brings unique aliveness to each individual Soul. Everyone is a unique and special person in the Spirit that created us all.

What Is God?

Question: What is God?
Answer: Everything.

About John–Roger

For the last 25 years, John-Roger has been deeply involved in working to promote greater health, well-being, and peace. He is the founder of the John-Roger Foundation, which supports a large number of organizations and individuals involved in education, science, health, and community service. The JRF is also the sponsor of the International Integrity Award, which is given annually to individuals who have demonstrated outstanding achievement in promoting individual and world peace.

In addition, John-Roger is the founder of Insight Transformational Seminars, which offers a range of seminars to enhance personal and professional effectiveness; Baraka Center, a healing and research clinic; Heartfelt Foundation, which is committed to community service; Koh-E-Nor University, a state-approved, degree-granting institution; Integrity Foundation, which is dedicated to promoting personal integrity; as well as other organizations committed to the same principles.

If you are interested in other books by John-Roger, write to Mandeville Press, P.O. Box 3935, Los Angeles, CA 90051, or call (213) 737-4055.